The Poet-Gardener: A Soul Care Model for Preaching

Guy R. Brewer

Copyright © 2009 by Guy R. Brewer
All rights reserved

CONTENTS

ACKNOWLEDGEMENTS	vi
INTRODUCTION	1
What Preaching Is and Is Not	4
The Poet-Gardener Model	16
Four Movements of the Spirit	18
MOVEMENT ONE: THE POET-GARDENER METAPHOR	19
The Means of Preaching: Life of the Heart	21
The Motive of Preaching: Transformation	23
The Method of Preaching: Inspired Personhood	27
Four Contexts of Poet-Gardener Preaching	29
Spiritual Formation Context: A Tri-Polar Model	29
Biblical Context: Preaching in Parables	31
Theological Context: Relational Theology	40
Social Context: Postmodern Worldview	49
MOVEMENT TWO: POETIC AND IMAGINATIVE ELEMENTS IN PREACHING	58
Four Hermeneutical Assumptions	61
Imagination: A Paradigm for Encountering God	62
Language and Grammar of Images	67
Imagination, Motivation, and the Volitional Life	69
Imagination and Epistemology	74
MOVEMENT THREE: SOUL CARE ELEMENTS IN PREACHING	83
Key terms for Soul Care Preaching	84
The Rhythm of Soul Care	97
The Anatomy of Decisions in Preaching	100
The Anatomy of Disciplines in Preaching	108
The Anatomy of Dispositions in Preaching	120
The Anatomy of Disciple-Making in Preaching	130
The Anatomy of Doxology in Preaching	155
MOVEMENT FOUR: IMAGES FOR POET-GARDENER PREACHING	159
Image One: Incarnational Presence	160

Image Two: The Wise Fool	171
Image Three: The Gardener	180
Image Four: The Poet	190

EPILOGUE 200

BIBLIOGRAPHY 207

ILLUSTRATIONS

Figures

	3-1	Components of Soul Care	87
	3-2	Three Movements of the Spiritual Life	95
	3-3	The Rhythm of Soul Care	97
	3-4	The Anatomy of Decisions	102
	3-6	The Web of Discipleship	133
	4-1	Rhythm of Attunement	167

Tables

	3-5	*METAMORPH* Soul Care Typology	126

ACKNOWLEDGMENTS

I thank my God every time I remember you (Philippians 1:3).

To paraphrase Chinua Achebe's famous proverb, it takes a whole community to write a book. As a matter of fact, some of the true joys in writing *Poet-Gardener* have been the many conversations and interactions with others that have informed this writing process. Much of writing is an isolated, even lonely, enterprise. The constant support of my wife and best friend, Rena, has allowed me the time to focus on writing. More than that, I have never felt alone because I knew that Rena was standing with me in this work. Due to her encouragement, I have been able to persevere. Rena, completion of this project is a success we share together.

Many others have been incarnations of God's grace to me in the course of this dissertation. Dr. David Sebastian has been more than an advisor. He has been a wise friend, colleague in ministry, and brother in the LORD throughout this process. I remain in his debt. And, I am very grateful to Anderson School of Theology for their financial support of this project. I could not have completed the work without their help.

At the risk of missing someone, I do want to acknowledge the generosity and helpfulness of a host of other persons. Dr. Janet Brewer has been incredibly helpful as a reviewer and coach on form and style. Members of the Nicholson Library staff, notably Barbara Hoover, provided invaluable research assistance along the way. Dr. Walter Breuggemann and Dr. Ellsworth Kalas have been treasured advisors and commentators. Dr. Betsy Muhlenfeld believed in me and this work from the beginning, providing me the time and resources to study at Oxford. My son and colleague in ministry, Jed Brewer, has provided critical input along the way. Jed, thanks for helping me keep it real. David

Neidert and Jan Schmidt have been generous partners to me, providing technical assistance. Amity Rees took my concept of a spiraling rhythm of soul care and developed the beautiful graphic that appears several times in the book. Her artistic contribution speaks for itself.

My students at Anderson School of Theology have been unwitting contributors to *Poet-Gardener*. As I have dialogued with them over the years, they have been marvelous teachers to me. Working with this community of emerging ministers has kept my ear to the ground of change and lived reality in the twenty-first century. I count it a great privilege and honor to be involved in raising up the next generation of Christian ministers.

First and last, I thank God for the countless acts of grace I have experienced in the course of writing this book. This project has formed me as much as I have formed it. My prayer is that God might use *Poet-Gardener* to build up the preaching ministry of the Church so that others might come to know the healing and love of Jesus Christ.

INTRODUCTION

Twenty-six years ago, a single sermon changed my life. In this spiritual experience, I could relate to John Wesley's characterization of his spiritual awakening at Aldersgate Street. To say the least, I had come "reluctantly" to hear this sermon.[1] The setting for the worship service was a drug and alcohol treatment facility in Bowling Green, Florida where I was a patient in a twenty-eight day program. My life was in deep crisis; I was a discouraged, hopeless person.

A young Lutheran minister came as a volunteer to the Bowling Green Inn each Thursday morning to conduct a worship service for those patients who wanted to attend. In actuality, we were offered a forced choice-the worship service or kitchen duty. I did not expect anything to happen at the worship service, but it was preferable to peeling potatoes.

Five or six of us gathered in a small room with the preacher and mumbled our way through a liturgy of prayers and half-hearted hymns. Then, the preacher read the Scripture, John 5:1-15. Although I had attended parochial schools for twelve years and had taken Bible courses in college, I could not recall having ever heard the story of the lame man at the pool of Bethesda.

When the preacher read Jesus' words, "Do you want to get well?" (John 5:6)[2], a mixture of conviction and curiosity stirred within me. I noticed that the young preacher seemed to stare at me as he read these words. Given my tenuous emotional state, I was easily offended. It seemed to me that he was singling me out of the crowd and meddling in my affairs.

---

[1] J. Ernest Rattenbury, *The Conversion of the Wesleys* (London: Epworth Press, 1938), 112.
[2] All Biblical references appear in New International Version (NIV) translation unless otherwise noted.

After the worship service, I confronted the preacher. "Why were you staring at me when you asked, 'Do you want to get well?' Do you think I'm some kind of moron?" He seemed shocked at my comment. "No, I don't think you are a moron and I wasn't staring at you. Those are the words of Jesus, not my own. Perhaps the LORD is trying to say something to you."

I dismissed the preacher's comments and went about my day. However, that question, "Do you want to get well?" haunted me. Of course, I wanted to get well. Why else would I agree to admission to an in-patient treatment program? Over the next few days I began to come to the realization that Jesus' question confronted the core of my problem. I wanted to drink more than I wanted to get well. What I lacked in my life was the "want power" to live a sober life.

The following Sunday, I asked permission to attend church services. The staff dropped me off at the Bowling Green United Methodist Church where the people welcomed me warmly. To my great shock, the preacher's sermon that morning focused on John 5:1-15, the story of the lame man at the pool of Bethesda. After the sermon, the pastor invited the congregation to meditate on the question, "Do you want to get well?" and to pray for healing. This became a converting, breakthrough moment for me.

I returned to the treatment program with a new found motivation and confidence to turn around my life. When I completed the twenty-eight day regimen, I returned to my hometown and family with hope and growing enthusiasm for a sober life. I had a lot of amends to make with folks I had harmed. And yet, I had a new found hope, a sense that God was leading me toward a future that I could not have asked or imagined.

In conversations with my pastor, I began to explore how I might serve my local church in a lay ministry. To my utter shock, Pastor Rittgers offered his discernment that God was calling me to vocational ministry. Such a suggestion seemed ludicrous. My family had endured major trauma over the past two years. The notion of uprooting them to go to seminary seemed out of the question. More than that, I struggled with deep shame about my sinful past.

I could not imagine that God could use such a frail and fallen person in pastoral leadership. Nonetheless, I agreed to explore the process of candidacy for ministry. In truly miraculous ways, one door after another opened for me to move my family, enter seminary, and begin serving the Church as a student pastor. Through all of these changes, my sense of God's presence with me grew. Truly, God was doing for me what I could not do for myself.

For the past twenty-five years, I have lived and ministered with the deep conviction that preaching makes a lasting difference in lives. A simple sermon that I heard unwillingly through the filter of despair changed my life. I believe that young, Lutheran pastor had no conception how God planned to use his volunteer ministry at Bowling Green Inn. He exercised obedience to preach the Word and God provided the results.

The Gospel of John refers to Jesus' miracles as signs, prophetic acts that point to the character and power of God.[3] Over many years, I have come to the conclusion that my healing is also a sign of God's compassion and power. My preaching is empowered by the inner testimony of God's miraculous work in my life. As such, I view every

---

[3] Raymond E Brown, *the Gospel of John, I-XII,* vol. 29 of the Anchor Bible (NY: Bantam Doubleday, 1966), 104-106.

sermon I preach as a personal testimony to God's living presence with us, whether I self-disclose my personal story or not.

At the same time that I have praised God for miraculous healing, my experience of healing and transformation through preaching has raised many questions in my mind. How did a simple sermon have such a profound effect in my life? What about faith dynamics? How could God have worked so powerfully in my life when I had so little faith and no confidence? What are the efficacious dynamics of soul care preaching? How does soul care preaching work in the internal processes of listeners to move people toward change? What is the role of the preacher and how can the preacher cooperate more intentionally with the work of the Holy Spirit? Is my personal experience of soul care preaching replicable? This book wrestles with these questions.

What Preaching Is and Is Not

My spiritual history, experience in ministry, and research point to five core convictions about preaching:

1. Preaching is essential to the health and vitality of the Church.
2. Preaching is an integral part of the Church's ministry of soul care.
3. Soul care preaching is a more accurate expression of Biblical ethos than rhetorical models for proclamation.
4. A poet-gardener model of preaching that emphasizes dynamics of inspiration and nurture is a Biblically grounded approach that speaks to the hearts of twenty-first century people.
5. Soul care preaching is an integrative enterprise, drawing upon elements of spirituality, theology, and the social sciences toward the goal of faithfulness in proclaiming God's Word.

As I reflect on the nature of preaching, St. Anselm's famous dictum comes to mind: "Fides quaerens intellectum," that is, faith seeking understanding.[4] The fact that

---

[4] Thomas Williams, "Saint Anselm," in *The Stanford Encyclopedia of Philosophy (Fall 2008 edition)*, ed. Edward N. Zalta, http://plato.standford.edu/archives/fall2008/entries/anselm (accessed July 3, 2008).

preachers speak out of faith, in faith, and to nurture faith is the distinguishing dynamic that sets apart preaching from all other forms of oral communication. Christian preaching is more public faith than it is public speaking. As St. Paul put it, ""It is written, 'I have believed; therefore, I have spoken.' With that same spirit of faith we also believed and therefore speak" (2 Corinthians 4:13).

Likewise, faith in the work of the Holy Spirit is the starting point for this exploration of preaching. Along the way, *Poet-Gardener* seeks to add to the Church's understanding of how God works through preaching to care for the souls of individuals and the faith community. As much as this exploration relies upon faith, it is also grounded in reality. Effective soul care preaching faces many obstacles.

Of all the ministries of the Church, preaching may be the most widely maligned and misunderstood. "Don't preach at me" is a stock phrase in colloquial speech for confronting unwanted feedback, particularly comments of a moral or spiritual nature. And yet, the great irony is that preaching is highly prized by laity and clergy alike.

In *The Great American Sermon Survey,* Lori Carrell interviewed 581 preachers and congregations representing a broad cross-section of Christian traditions. In response to the question, "What component of the church service has the most impact on your life?" thirty-five percent of lay respondents ranked the sermon as highest impact (35%) followed by communion (20%) and prayer (18%).[5] In a related survey item, "Rank order your ministerial tasks in order of importance," 43% of clergy ranked sermon preparation as first priority.[6]

---

[5] Lori Carrell, *The Great American Sermon Survey* (Wheaton, IL: Mainstay Church Resources, 2000), 95.
[6] Ibid., 119.

Despite the fact that folks in the pew and the pulpit value preaching highly, the chorus of complaints that preaching is boring, irrelevant, and ineffective continues. How can this be? The ministry of preaching labors under the burden of several persistent myths and misconceptions that contribute to ineffectiveness of sermons. These myths and misconceptions include:

1. The bifurcation of preaching and the pastoral care ministry of the Church.
2. The psychologically based assumption that pastoral preaching is an exercise in problem solving or religious coping.
3. The dominant and long standing model of preaching as a performance. More specifically, models of preaching as rhetoric or public speech directed toward persuasion predominate the training and practice of pulpit ministers.
4. The notion that preaching is primarily an educational enterprise, designed to transmit spiritual truth or religious information.
5. The postmodern rejection of preaching, including the term, "preaching," as an irrelevant anachronistic practice of an out of touch institutional church.

In every area of human endeavor, specialization equates with competence and sophistication. This is no less true of ministry. A cursory review of seminary curricula points to specialized training of ministers in Biblical languages, Scriptural exegesis, systematic theology, ethics, pastoral care, and preaching. By necessity, the training process is sharply focused on subject areas, at times treating each specialized domain of ministry as a free standing practice.[7]

The problem arises when ministers unreflectively carry this compartmentalization of ministry into their practice in a local congregation. Pastoral care is often viewed as activity other than preaching that the minister does to care for the hurts and needs of parishioners throughout the week. What happens on Sunday, the worship life of the congregation, and particularly, preaching, becomes a separate and disconnected part of ministry.

---

[7] Charles R. Foster et al., *Educating Clergy: Teaching Practices and Pastoral Imagination* (San Francisco: Jossey-Bass, 2006), 40.

It is little wonder that congregations view preaching as irrelevant to their lives in churches where the preacher has implicitly decided that the preached Word is not a part of caring for the lives or the souls of congregants. The emphasis in the worship experience can easily become other-worldly, disconnected from this-world problems and concerns of people. Where the congregation remains unaware that Christian worship is a primary act of pastoral care that calls us to return to our roots as a covenantal community, preaching becomes the "preacher's thing" in which listeners feel little ownership.[8]

A related misconception envisions pastoral care as a one-on-one, private ministry in which the pastor ministers to individuals. Indeed, many acts of pastoral care are highly personal, sensitive, and confidential conversations with the pastor. However, a privatistic model ignores Jesus' emphasis on community as the locus of care: "By this all men will know that you are my disciples, if you love one another" (John 13:35). An important function of preaching is to call, inspire, and empower the community of faith to undertake its vital role of care for one another.[9]

The temptation is quite strong to reduce preaching to good advice and teaching on how to cope with life in a spiritual way. Television network schedules are full of programs, ranging from "Dr. Phil" to "Dr. Oz," dedicated to giving people real life solutions to their problems. And, church reader boards across America advertise a plethora of "how to" sermons as the weekly spiritual diet. Church pews are full of people seeking answers to complex, painful life situations. As compassionate persons, pastors want to help their congregants find solutions to their problems.

---

[8] William H Willimon, *Pastor: The Theology and Practice of Ordained Ministry* (Nashville: Abingdon Press, 2002), 75-90.

[8] Margaret Kornfeld, *Cultivating Wholeness: A Guide to Care and Counseling in Faith Communities* (New York: Continuum, 2006), 84.

Many scholars in psychology of religion support this notion of religion as problem solving. More precisely, religious practice is often equated with coping skills. Kenneth Pargament posits that all religious behavior can be mapped in terms of four pathways of coping including strategies of preservation, reconstruction, re-valuation, and re-creation.[10] Pargament's schema suggests that religious interventions, including preaching, provide people with a holding environment in which core values are clarified, strengthened, and protected. At the same time, he suggests religious practice provides a pathway to change, even radical transformation, through reframing of cognitive and volitional processes. Such psychologically-based constructs provide helpful maps to human religious behavior. However, they run the risk of reductionist thinking that leaves no room for the work of the Holy Spirit.

The popularity of "how to" sermons arises from the desire of preachers to deliver messages that respond to the felt needs of the congregation. Psychologically based notions of self-help and human agency lie behind this approach. In particular, much current preaching targeted toward felt needs operates from the assumption that people know best what they need and want.[11] Even more insidious, such approaches betray an arrogant impulse toward prescription of divine activity in human life. In other words, much of therapeutic or life application preaching relies upon the human community to set the agenda or goals for sermons.

As much as psychologized models of preaching encounter problems with misguided goals or end points, such models also run the risk of building upon human

---

[10] Kenneth Pargament,. *The Psychology of Religion and Coping: Theory, Research, and Practice* (New York: Guilford Press, 2001), 111.
[11] Jim Shaddix, *The Passion-Driven Sermon: Changing the Way Pastors Preach and Congregations Listen* (Nashville: Broadman and Holman, 2003), 84-85.

starting points to the exclusion of God's agenda. Richard Niebuhr's typology of theological integration includes a "Christ of culture" polarity in which the teachings of Christ are inextricably intertwined with cultural categories.[12] Preachers who operate with extreme forms of "Christ of culture" presuppositions see the sermon as the application of the best of human understanding to the cause of Christ. The problem arises when preaching silences God's agenda, leaving little to no room for God's revelation.

Drawing upon Niebuhr's typology, the poet-gardener model relies upon a "Christ transforming culture," hierarchical integration in which the preacher respects the value of wisdom from human sources while relying upon God's revelation as the primary and interpretive source of wisdom.[13] Here is a relational model of truth; to know the truth is to know the Person who is the way, the truth, and the life. For the poet-gardener, preaching that limits proclamation to problem solving or training in coping skills falls short of an adequate model for soul care preaching through which the Word becomes flesh.

From ancient times, the Church has struggled with a confusion of preaching with rhetoric. In Paul's first letter to the church at Corinth, he addresses this misconception. As people immersed in a Greek culture that highly prized persuasive speech, the young congregation at Corinth found themselves enamored with Apollos, a recent convert with significant training and gifts in rhetoric. In response to controversy in the church over

---

[12] Richard H. Niebuhr, *Christ and Culture* (Harper and Brothers Publishers, New York, 1951), 39-44.
[12] Ibid, 39-44.

preaching, Paul asserts his own calling to preach "not with words of human wisdom" (1 Corinthians 1:17).[14]

Obviously, preaching is speech. However, theological problems arise when the Church equates preaching with rhetoric or public speaking. Paul clearly differentiates public speech from preaching in the way he characterizes his own message: "I came to you in weakness and fear, and with much trembling. My message and my preaching were not with wise and persuasive words, but with a demonstration of the Spirit's power" (1 Corinthians 2:1-3). He intentionally rejects the notion that preaching ignites faith based upon the persuasiveness of the preacher: "That your faith might not rest on men's wisdom, but on God's power" (1 Corinthians 2:5). When Paul preached, he went public with his faith. For him, proclamation was the mediation of a relationship with the risen LORD.

When preachers conceive of sermons as public speaking performances with religious language and purposes, they find themselves tempted to focus on personal effort, mechanics of speech, and dynamics of persuasion. These facets of preaching easily become idols. When anxiety about personal adequacy and fear of failure are added to the mix, the preacher suffers from cognitive and spiritual dissonance, an inner duplicity in which the focus of the sermon oscillates between God's agenda and narcissism.[15] By contrast, Paul characterizes his own preaching as the antithesis of rhetoric: "I did not come with eloquence or superior wisdom as I proclaimed to you God's power."[16] He is

---

[14] C.K. Barrett, *The First Epistle to Corinthians* (Peabody, MA: Hendrickson Publishers, 1993), 41-43.
[15] Fred B. Craddock, Preaching (Nashville: Abingdon Press, 2010), *22-30*.
[16] C.K. Barrett, *The First Letter to the Corinthians,* 41-43.

unconcerned about the persuasiveness of his speech because he is thoroughly convinced of the efficacy of the Holy Spirit working through the Word to change human hearts.

The poet-gardener affirms the servant role of the preacher as one who relies upon God's inspiration to nurture faith and transformation. The preacher assumes that he or she plays a secondary role, leaving the primary burden of communication to Christ. For the poet-gardener, faithfulness is the steady drum beat of preaching. As Paul asserted, Christ is the only foundation on whom all those who proclaim the Word are building.[17]

Because preaching involves public speech, a primary theological challenge arises in questions related to authority. By what authority does the preacher speak? Does the preacher's authority arise from her or his position or skill as a pulpit minister? Is the source of authority that of a beloved pastor whom the congregation trusts and admires? Is the preacher's authority that of the oracle, one who speaks the very words of God?

Homiletical models that emphasize rhetoric and persuasion fail to adequately clarify the nature of authority of the preacher. Poet-gardener offers a tri-polar perspective of preaching that conceives the act of proclamation as holy speech arising from love of God, love of neighbor, and love of self. The poet-gardener draws authority to preach from agape love.

A renowned Biblical scholar recently presented a series of lectures on Pauline writings at the seminary where I teach. In reflecting on these presentations, I asked students: "Would you characterize these presentations as sermons?" Students' responses were far ranging. Those immersed in traditions that value "teaching" sermons and who hold the Scriptures in high esteem responded "yes"-certainly these Bible-centered talks were sermons. Students who embrace a relational theology felt equally strongly in the

---

[17] C.K. Barrett, 42..

opposite direction. They characterized the presentations as scholarly, edifying lectures, but not sermons.

Teaching models that overemphasize didactic content in sermons to the exclusion of connection with the listeners miss the mark in fulfilling the ministry of preaching. Without a doubt, congregations need Biblical teaching. Pastors are legitimately concerned about the growing Biblical illiteracy in congregations. Sunday school participation is at an all-time low in many churches. When pastors conceive of the Sunday morning sermon as the principal, perhaps the only, opportunity for people to learn the Bible, they have come to a natural conclusion: teaching the Word is the priority task of the sermon.

However, preaching is much more than the dissemination of information, even information about the Bible. In many ways, the manner in which the preacher approaches the teaching function is a theological decision. Those who emphasize the teaching role of the preacher often build upon developmental learning theory. From their point of view, sermons are opportunities to pour vital information into the lives of people. In keeping with much of secular educational theory, the implicit assumption is that people will make better choices in life if they have better information. In this mindset of "scientia," knowledge becomes the x-factor that will make the difference in people's lives.[18]

On the other hand, the Scriptures reject knowledge in and of itself as spiritually edifying: "Knowledge puffs up, but love builds up" (1 Corinthians 8:1). Jesus speaks of wisdom, "sapientia," and invites the community of faith to a personal relationship with

---

[18] Eugene H. Peterson and Marva Dawn, *The Unnecessary Pastor: Rediscovering the Call* (Grand Rapids, MI: William B. Eerdmans, 2000), 121-138.

Him as the pathway of spiritual learning: "Take my yoke upon you and learn from me, for I am gentle and humble in heart, and you will find rest for your souls" (Matthew 11:29). To be wise is more than knowing facts about Jesus or memorizing Bible passages. The fount of wisdom is fear of the LORD, the educative dimension of personal relationship with God through Jesus Christ.[19]

A key quality for effective preaching is diligent study. Quite naturally, a preacher who has studied the Scriptures for years has developed not only an impressive body of knowledge, but also a keen desire to share that knowledge with others. One of the most difficult processes for preachers is paring down the huge body of information from the week's study into a sermon. In translating the study process into the pulpit, each preacher must ask herself or himself, "What do the people need to know? What should I teach from this Scripture?"[20]

The poet-gardener relies upon the Biblical affirmation that the Holy Spirit is the teacher of the faith community. As such, the sermon study process goes beyond the notion of "getting up a sermon" in favor of obediently listening for a word of wisdom from God. The preacher seeks to be part of God's incarnational presence, embracing the promise of Jesus to send the Spirit of truth who will "teach you all things and will remind you of everything I have said to you" (John 14:25). In this sense, preaching is education in the original meaning of the Latin root, "educare," which means to "draw out." The

---

[19] Eugene Peterson and Marva Dawn, *The Unnecessary Pastor,* 121-138.
[20] Fred B. Craddock, Preaching, 37-40.
[21] Henri Nouwen, *Creative Ministry* (New York: Image Books, 1991), 12-14.

poet-gardener seeks to draw out that which God has already worked into the heart of the faith community.[21]

A growing trend in twenty-first century consciousness draws a sharp divide between religion and spirituality. Increasingly, religion equates with institutional categories and forms that conjure largely negative images. By contrast, a host of authors from secular as well as faith tradition perspectives portray spirituality as an inherent human need to connect with the "more than." Spirituality is becoming the term of choice for authentic practice related to expression of faith.[22]

The ministry of preaching finds itself caught in the crossfire of this shift in thinking about religious and spiritual practice. Many persons, particularly those influenced by the emerging church movement, view preaching as an anachronistic practice perpetuated by the tradition of the Church. Even the term, "preaching," has acquired negative connotations. Emerging church authors such as Dan Kimball describe traditional preaching as an aberration of authentic Christian practice which fractures community.[23]

What's at stake in the minds of these authors is the community process of meaning making. For them, the traditional model of one person preaching from a pulpit to the community relies upon an outmoded notion of hierarchy where the minister is in charge. Emerging church theology rejects the notion of the preacher speaking for the community. Instead, postmodern thinking offers the alternatives of shared discernment

---

[22] Walter Principe, "Toward Defining Spirituality." in *Exploring Christian Spirituality: An Ecumenical Reader* ed. Kenneth J. Collins (Grand Rapids, MI: Baker Academic, 2000), 43-60.
[23] Dan Kimball, *The Emerging Church: Vintage Christianity for New Generations* (Grand Rapids, MI: Zondervan, 2003), 171-196.

and shared meaning in which all community members have equal authority. In this mindset, preaching becomes a dialogue.[24]

Objections to preaching arise from logic founded on both theological and contextual rationales. In theological terms, emerging church thinkers contend that modern preaching has deviated in substantive ways from the New Testament model of "kerygma," the faithful proclamation of God's message. These same authors contend that the nature of communication has shifted in the twenty-first century. People no longer rely upon authority figures for important information, let alone for permission to think or act. In all forms of human communities, the leadership "pyramid" has been replaced by the level playing field. Effective communication in postmodern thinking involves egalitarian conversation.[25]

The poet-gardener engages in a homiletical approach that is both Biblically faithful and culturally sensitive to twenty-first century categories. In significant ways he or she seeks to reclaim the Church's devotion to "kerygma," the widely used New Testament term for preaching. C.H. Dodd characterizes kerygma as inclusive of the following elements:

1. Preaching that embodies the fulfillment of God's promises through the prophets, per Jesus' inaugural sermon at Nazareth (Luke 4:14-21).
2. Preaching empowered through the presence of the resurrected LORD.
3. Preaching anointed through the power of the Holy Spirit, empowering Jesus' followers to be witnesses throughout the world (Acts 1:8).
4. Preaching energized by the expectation of Jesus' return and consummation of the age (Matthew 28:20).
5. Preaching that urgently appeals for a response of repentance with the offer of God's forgiveness, salvation, and life in the Spirit.[26]

---

24 Dan Kimball, *The Emerging Church, 171-196.*
[25] Ibid.
[26]C.H. Dodd, *The Apostolic Preaching and Its Developments: Three Lectures with an Eschatology and History* (New York: Harper and Row, 1964).

The way in which the poet-gardener might preach a call to repentance provides a case in point for his or her distinctive style of proclamation. The preacher avoids beginning with a rehearsal of the sins of the people and the perils of rebellion in the style of Jonathan Edwards' "Sinners in the Hands of an Angry God."[27] Such an approach runs the risk of rejection without a hearing. To the conditioned ear of postmodern listeners, rehearsals of eternal damnation come across as judgmental fear tactics. Instead, the poet-gardener starts with self-disclosure of her or his own fallenness. He or she invites the people to move together in praying, "LORD, we repent. Let repentance begin with me."

In subsequent chapters, this book explores elements of postmodern culture which present a challenge to preaching. A primary contextual debate revolves around the nature of authority and how any person derives the authority to preach the Gospel. On a related note, postmodern thinking raises fundamental questions about the locus of truth and the process of spiritual discernment. The other critical piece to the puzzle is the postmodern notion of community. Twenty-first century people perceive genuine intimacy within the faith community as the primary metric of authenticity of the Church.

The Poet-Gardener Model

The poet gardener model is a response to the foregoing challenges to effective preaching. It should be noted at the start that the poet-gardener seeks to avoid a polemical or argumentative tone against other forms or styles of preaching. Instead, the poet-gardener model affirms that the preaching ministry of the Church has room for many

---

27Jonathan Edwards, *Sinners in the Hands of an Angry God* (Pensacola, FL: Christian Life Books, 2003).

distinct voices that share a common love of Christ and devotion to the truth of the Bible. Moreover, these reflections do not purport to be flawless or without many growing edges. The poet-gardener preaches with the faith Paul articulated, "The important thing is that in every way, whether from false motives or true, Christ is preached" (Philippians 1:18).

The poet-gardener speaks in a voice that is distinctive but not original. Robert Webber suggests in *Ancient Future Church: Rethinking Evangelicalism for a Post-Modern World* that twenty-first century folks are finding spiritual awakening as they rediscover apostolic tradition, including ancient forms of preaching.[28] The poet-gardener endeavors to be faithful to the orthodox tradition of the Church while sensitively embracing forms and styles of proclamation that will make a connection with the hearts and minds of postmodern people.

To define the term, poet-gardener, this exploration offers several angles of vision that substantiate the legitimacy and helpfulness of this metaphor. In particular, the case is made for the importance of the dyadic character of the poet-gardener approach: Seeking to inspire and nurture congregations as co-equal goals of preaching. In pursuit of these goals, the poet-gardener weaves together insights from communication studies, Biblical scholarship, theology of preaching, and sociology.

The underlying presupposition is that Western culture has shifted on a meta-scale to a postmodern worldview that incorporates new ground rules for making meaning. As such, the poet-gardener model seeks to approach preaching in a way that provides a pathway to the Gospel in accessible language that does not experiment with or alter the core confessions of Christian faith.

---

[28] Robert E. Webber, *Ancient-Future Faith: Rethinking Evangelicalism for a Postmodern World* (Grand Rapids, MI: Baker Academic, 1999), 13-42.

Four Movements of the Spirit

A major premise of the poet-gardener model is that preaching involves two streams of influence on listeners:

1. A poetic dynamic that seeks to inspire the congregation.
2. A gardener dynamic that seeks to nurture individuals and the congregation.

This book is comprised of four movements that build a case for these twin tasks of preaching. Characterizing these reflections as a pattern of movements already discloses a central assumption of poet-gardener. That is, poet-gardener preaching is an exercise of public faith in which the preacher and the congregation seek to move in harmony with the Spirit of God. Taken as a whole, this model for preaching is offered as a choreography for the Church to joyfully dance with God.

Effective sermons demand that the preacher understand not only the Bible text, but also the spiritual, theological, and social contexts of the setting. In the first movement, the book explores these four critical contexts for preaching. In the second movement, *The Poet-Gardener* reflects on the question: How might a faith community encounter God in imaginative as well as cognitive ways? Movement Three offers an in-depth model for soul care in preaching. The final movement of *The Poet-Gardener* offers the reader four images of preaching that resonate with postmodern listeners.

Source: Lavinia Fontana (1581), "Jesus appears to Mary Magdalene."

MOVEMENT ONE: THE POET-GARDENER METAPHOR

The LORD God took the man and put him in the Garden of Eden to work it and take care of it (Genesis 2:15).

For we are God's workmanship (poiema), *created in Christ Jesus to do good works which God prepared in advance for us to do* (Ephesians 2:10).

From the generation of Adam, human beings have been poet-gardeners. The creation account pictures the first humans as God's personal gardeners in Eden endowed with a purpose in life. God gave humans the gift of meaningful work that produces fruit.

Paul reiterates the theological truth that humans were created with a vocation, but he adds an additional dimension. Not only were we created to do good work, we are also God's "*poiema*," God's own workmanship. Drawing from the root word, we are literally God's poetry. As poets, our imaginative, creative efforts reflect the mind and heart of the Creator.

The poet-gardener metaphor also builds on reflections from literature in Christian leadership development. Tim Elmore coined the term, "poet-gardener," in his reflections on leadership in the twenty-first century. In *A New Kind of Leader: Leading Effectively as Our Culture Evolves,* Elmore offers a typology of shifting paradigms for leadership in American society. Within this typology, he suggests that the emerging postmodern culture requires a more relational, creative approach to leadership which he dubs, "poet gardener."[29] This study builds upon Elmore's poet-gardener metaphor and expands the concept to Christian preaching.

One might examine the anatomy of poet-gardener preaching by asking three questions:

1. What are the *means* of preaching?
2. What is the *motive* of preaching?

---

[29] Tim Elmore, "A New Kind of Leader: Leading Effectively as Our Culture Evolves," Growing Leaders, http:// www.growingleaders.com (accessed July 2, 2008), 1-5.

3. What is the *method* of preaching?

The Means of Preaching: Life of the Heart

The poet-gardener metaphor points to both a way of being a disciple and a way of preaching. The preacher operates with the conviction that proclamation is an overflow of the heart: "Out of the overflow of his heart his mouth speaks" (Luke 6:45). In other words, the preacher's first concern in the ministry of proclamation is the condition of his or her heart. The poet-gardener affirms that all sermons are "from the heart" to the good or ill of the listeners. As Dennis Kinlaw reflects, "The greatest problem in preaching is not the preparation of the sermon but the preparation of the preacher."[30]

Making claim to speak from the heart is both a strength and a challenge to the poet-gardener. One might easily slip into a radical subjectivism in which any point of view is self-justified as a heartfelt impulse. Something more is needed. Where does the poet-gardener find authority to preach?

If the well-spring of inspiration for the poet-gardener is overflow of the heart, authority to preach is a derived, two-pronged authority. The preacher draws authority from God's calling: "You did not choose me, but I chose you and appointed you to go and bear fruit-fruit that will last" (John 15:16). Henri Nouwen speaks of God-given authority to preach in terms of "being taken."[31] The poet-gardener preaches with the conviction that God has taken hold of his or her ministry to guide and empower proclamation.

---

[30] Dennis F. Kinlaw, *Preaching in the Spirit,* 17.
[31] Henri Nouwen, *Life of the Beloved: Spiritual Living in a Secular World* (New York: Crossroads, 2003), 43.

Even as the poet-gardener relies upon God's calling to authorize preaching, he or she draws a second source of authority from the blessing of the Church.[32] The preacher does not stand over the people but comes from the community to speak on behalf of the community. He or she articulates shared faith with the listeners as they seek together a fresh encounter with God. The poet-gardener eschews the flawed image of chief executive of the Church. Rather, the preacher speaks as a baptized member of the laity. The Church validates gifts for proclamation and blesses the preacher who stands to share a word from God.[33]

The poet-gardener embraces the conviction that ministry is more about relationships than tasks. As such, relational connection is the communicative means of preaching. Before it is public speech or the communication of information, preaching is a conversation among friends.[34] The preacher seeks to be present with the people without anxiety about accomplishing a "to do" list in the sermon. Leaving the results of the sermon to God, he or she joins the people in expectantly waiting upon the LORD for wisdom and grace.

The poet-gardener expresses his or her priority on connectivity through genuine love for people and for God. Healthy curiosity and the desire to learn about the worldview and culture of others spring from genuine love. With the knowledge that love grows as one gets to know another more intimately, the poet-gardener eagerly seeks to know the questions, hopes, and fears of the people to whom she or he preaches. Preparation to preach involves a "sacred triangle" in which the preacher brings together

---

[32] William H. Willimon, *Pastor: The Theology and Practice of Ordained Ministry*, 141-160.
[33] Ibid.
[34] Lucy Atkinson Rose, *Sharing the Word: Preaching in the Roundtable Church* (Louisville: Westminster John Knox, 1997), 121.

three loves: a love of the people to whom one preaches, a love of Christ, and a love for the task of preaching.[35]

Before the first word is uttered, the poet-gardener is committed to listening carefully to God, to his or her own heart, and to the community of faith. The preacher acts as an articulator of inner events who gives language to the deep yearnings of the heart.[36] Such a role requires active listening, contemplation, and discernment. Equally, the poet-gardener recognizes that the congregation willingly hears a word from the pulpit when they sense that they have been heard. As Henri Nouwen puts it, the preacher speaks in such a way that the people respond, "Yes, I have felt exactly like that, but I never had the words for it!"[37]

A final means for the poet-gardener is hopefulness. Relying upon the faithfulness and sovereignty of God, the preacher claims the promise of Jesus: "My Father is always at his work to this very day, and I, too, am working" (John 5:17). This emphasis on hopefulness in preaching recognizes that hope is both the motivational keystone of change and a vital gift that the faith community offers to the world.[38] Without lapsing into a Pollyannaish worldview that denies the reality of suffering in the life of the congregation, the poet-gardener preaches with the conviction that no one is beyond redemption and no relationships are beyond reconciliation.

The Motive of Preaching: Transformation

Nothing is more frustrating to the preacher than delivering a sermon that falls flat, seemingly having no impact on the listeners. In fact, the point of sermons is change,

---

[35] Ellsworth J. Kalas, *Preaching from the Soul* (Nashville: Abingdon, 2003), 27-34.
[36] Henri Nouwen, *Creative Ministry,* 21-40.
[37] Ibid.
[38] Everett L. Worthington, *Forgiving and Reconciling: Bridges to Wholeness and Hope* (Downers Grove, IL: InterVarsity, 2003), 47-72.

qualitative life change in which people are moving toward conformation into the image of Christ. Such genuine transformation involves a change of heart, a seismic shift in the inner core of persons.

At the same time the poet-gardener's motive for preaching is transformation, he or she acknowledges powerlessness to effect such change. But all things are possible with God. God works in transformative ways through the love of the preacher for the people. In a fundamental sense, preaching is a word of agape love with the potential to change lives.

The poet-gardener speaks as a friend of Jesus and child of God. The motivation to call others into a genuine relationship with God arises from the preacher's intimacy with God. In a sense, the sermon invites listeners into God's circle of close friends. Regardless of the content of the sermon, the tone includes elements of genuine intimacy with Christ. Preaching is a relational connection before it becomes an educational or rhetorical experience.[39]

Since poet-gardener preaching seeks transformation of the core self, the primary locus of sermons is the life of the heart. The poet-gardener is not content to preach in ways that appeal only to the intellect. Likewise, he or she is not simply seeking an emotional response from the congregation. The point of preaching for the poet-gardener is to connect the heart of the congregation with the heart of God. As Henri Nouwen suggests, the beginning point of Christian discipleship is when a person hears the message from God, "You are my beloved."[40]

---

[39] Burton Z. Cooper and John S. McClure, *Claiming Theology in the Pulpit,* 10-11.
[40] Henri Nouwen, *Life of the Beloved,* 4.

The poet-gardener understands transformation in terms of holistic formation. To be conformed to the image of Christ includes profound change in all dimensions of human functioning. Avoiding the temptation to force change or foist his or her agenda on others, the preacher seeks to help listeners catch a God-given vision for their lives. And yet, the preacher must avoid confusing human freedom with autonomy. Contrary to popular psychological notions, the point of personal growth is not development of the ability to independently meet one's own needs. Transformational sermons deal in the truth of the human condition that entails dependence on God and interdependence in the community. For the poet-gardener, to empower others is to connect them in a vital way with the power and love of God that flow from the community of faith.[41]

An important quality of the poet-gardener in facilitating transformation is openness. At the same time he or she is highly motivated to facilitate transformation in others, the preacher remains open to God's timing and ways in bringing about change. On a human level, openness to meet others where they are in life is a prerequisite to effecting change. The poet-gardener has an authentic interest in others and values their distinctive cultures and contributions. He or she practices attentiveness to the intuitive worldview and presuppositional foundations of people, what Clarissa Pinkola Estes refers to as "The river beneath the river."[42]

It is vitally important that those who preach be self-aware of personal prejudices and biases in order to avoid favoritism or exclusion of diverse points of view. Openness to those who are different or even offensive to the prevailing church culture requires a non-defensiveness in which the preacher is able to let go of the need to correct or control

---

[41] Tim Elmore. Tim. *A New Kind of Leader: Leading Effectively as Our Culture Evolves*, 1-7.
[42] Clarissa Pinkola Estes,. *Women Who Run with the Wolves* (New York: Ballantine, 1996), 22-23.

others. Such openness is empowered by a healthy core self, what McMinn refers to as the "triangle of wholeness." In this concept McMinn points to the need for an accurate sense of self, an accurate sense of need, and openness to relationships.[43] To the degree that the poet-gardener possesses these balances, he or she is able to see the beautiful potential in others beneath the veneer of deformative coping behaviors.

The poet-gardener proactively promotes a climate of hospitality where people have the freedom and safety to grow, develop, and change. In this vein, he or she seeks to influence others by attraction rather than promotion. Poet-gardener sermons do not simply include an invitation and altar call at the end of the sermon in the fashion of evangelistic sermons. Rather, they are an invitation to join God's company in a safe community where one is valued as a person and provided room to grow.[44]

Building bridges of spiritual experience is the focal point of preaching. Drawing upon imaginative and intuitive processes, the preacher synthesizes and extrapolates from the market place of ideas in the social context to provide spiritual links for the congregation. The poet-gardener brings together the timeless Word of God with the temporal concerns of people through the bridge of words spoken in love. In the language of Tim Elmore, the preacher seeks to communicate "big picture ideas" by merging thoughts with feelings and intuitions in poetic form.[45] The goal here is to bring together the longings and hopes of the people with the incarnational presence of Christ.

Relational connection is fundamental to the poet-gardener model because the primary goal in soul care preaching is to develop people. The preacher aims for "inside-

---

[43] Mark McMinn, *Psychology, Theology, and Spirituality in Christian Counseling* (Philadelphia: Tyndale, 1996), 29-60.
[44] Henri Nouwen, *Reaching Out: The Three Movements of the Spiritual Life* (New York: Image, 1971), 65-78.
[45] Tim Elmore, *Leading Effectively: A New Kind of Leader as Our Culture Evolves*, 1-7.

out" change with particular attention to the core self, the heart. She or he views preaching as a means of pastoral care, a vital part of spiritual formation of individuals and the community as a whole.[46]

Lastly, the preacher builds on confidence in the efficacy of the Word of God to transform lives. However, God rarely speaks in an audible voice. The poet-gardener preaches as a partner with God in translating the *logos,* the eternal Word of God for all humanity, into a *rhema,* a personal word from God to particular people at specific times and places. As David Yonggi Cho suggests, the experience of the *rhema* is the "fourth dimension" of life in which the experience of the Holy Spirit works a new creation.[47]

The Method of Preaching: Inspired Personhood

At a recent academic presentation, I was surprised by the style of introduction of the principal speaker. "Today's presenter is a disciple of Jesus Christ," the introduction began. Here is the heart of the poet-gardener. His or her identity grows out of vital relationship with Jesus Christ rather than credentials, titles, or roles. The sense of security and confidence of the preacher arises from assurance in God's calling and dependence on God's provision.

How does the poet-gardener develop and nurture a priority on personal discipleship at the core of his or her personhood? Here, the preacher is a living paradox. On the one hand, he or she communicates a sense of security and personal authority. On the other hand, the poet-gardener assiduously avoids the arrogance of self-reliance. As

---

[46] Lawrence J. Crabb, *Inside-Out* (Colorado Springs, CO: NavPress, 2007), 27-42.
[47] David Yonggi Cho, *The Fourth Dimension, Volume II* (Gainesville, FL: Bridge-Logos, 2002), 35-37.

John Ortberg suggests, Christian discipleship requires the discipline of smallness, intentional obscurity and unobtrusiveness.[48]

The poet-gardener places high value on accurate self-awareness. At the same time the preacher ministers out of God's grace and affirmation, she or he has a profound awareness of his or her shadow side and personal woundedness. For the poet-gardener, sermons that call for repentance and reconciliation are autobiographical messages at some level. In keeping with Henri Nouwen's reflections in *The Wounded Healer,* he or she finds hope in the paradox of the cross in which God converts wounds into a source of healing and redemption.[49]

The poet-gardener uses personhood as a vital element in preaching in two important ways. With an understanding of systemic dynamics in her or his pastoral leadership, the preacher practices a non-anxious presence in the pulpit. Working intentionally to keep anxiety levels low in the faith community is a critical contribution of the preacher in building a nurturing environment. The way in which she or he is present with the congregation sets the emotional and spiritual tone for the community. As such, the poet-gardener models a confidence in God and trust of the congregation that is contagious.[50]

A second important use of personhood for the poet-gardener is intentional transparency. The critical dynamic here is appropriate self-disclosure. Drawing upon self-awareness of his or her motives and emotional needs, the preacher discloses doubts and failures as well as faith and victories. The poet-gardener understands the power of

---

[48] John Ortberg, *The Life You've Always Wanted* (Grand Rapids, MI: Zondervan, 2002), 130-131.
[49] Henri Nouwen, *The Wounded Healer* (New York: Doubleday, 1979), 79-96.
[50] Ronald Richardson, *Creating a Healthier Church: Family Systems Theory* (Philadelphia: Fortress Press, 1996), 41-53.

authenticity in building connections with people. He or she seeks to be a real person among other real persons who are seeking a genuine relationship with God. In keeping with the principle of transparency, Mark McMinn suggests that the preacher ask herself or himself: "What kind of self-disclosure with what motives and under what circumstances will be most helpful to the congregation?"[51]

Four Contexts of Poet-Gardener Preaching

Spiritual Formation Context: A Tri-polar Model

Jesus summed up the spiritual life by drawing upon the words of the Torah. Quoting the "Shema" (Deuteronomy 6:4, 5), he pointed to the "first and greatest commandment:" "You shall love the Lord your God with all your heart and with all your soul and with all your mind" (Matthew 22:37). Note that Jesus did not stop with this mono-polar definition of spirituality. Instead, he proceeded to add second and third dimensions to the spiritual equation in the words of Leviticus 19:18: "Love your neighbor as yourself."(Matthew 22:39). Poet-gardeners rely upon the tri-polar spirituality expressed in these words of Jesus.

David Augsburger offers an incisive analysis of Christian spirituality in which he describes tri-polar spirituality:

> "Tri-polar spirituality is the breakthrough in which love of God transcends and transforms love of self, love of God and love of neighbor become one, love of neighbor and love of self become one, and submission to God and solidarity with neighbor are indivisible."[52]

In Augsburger's model, Christian spirituality consists of three interdependent dimensions that are inseparable. To live in the Spirit is to experience God's love as upwardly directed in compliance to the will of God. But equally, the spiritual life is

---

[51] Mark McMinn, *Psychology, Theology, and Spirituality in Counseling,* 48-49.
[52] David Augsburger, *Dissident Discipleship*, 13.

inwardly directed as appropriate self-regard and outwardly moving in compassion for other people. Because each movement of the Spirit is interwoven with the other two, living an authentically Christian spiritual life cannot be compartmentalized into Sunday morning experience. To be Christian is an experience of immersion in the love of God in every facet of being and doing.[53]

The spiritual formation context for the poet-gardener is a unified, tri-polar spirituality that invites the congregation to a holistic experience of God. Sermons in this model may not degenerate to a mirror-of-self spirituality in which we create God in our own image. Likewise, the poet-gardener does not settle for preaching a message that stops at inviting congregants to a personal relationship with Christ characterized merely as "My Jesus and me." Drawing upon a tri-polar spirituality, the preacher confronts consumerist and pietistic notions of relationship with God. As an alternative, he or she offers Jesus' example of radical obedience to God that requires laying down your life for your friends.[54]

Henri Nouwen also spoke of the spiritual life in terms of three movements: the movement from isolation to solitude, the movement from hostility to hospitality, and the movement from illusion to prayer. The operative word in Nouwen's proposal is movement. He emphasizes the notion that spiritual experience is never a goal or credential to be achieved. Rather, Nouwen asserts that all humans have trouble staying the course of spiritual growth. The movement of the spiritual life is more a wave pattern, vacillating between poles of connection and alienation, grace and fallenness.[55]

---

[53] Ibid.
[54] Ibid.,15-16.
[55] Henri Nouwen, *Reaching Out: The Three Movements of the Spiritual Life,* 3-9.

Nouwen's model is helpful in offering a combination of realism and grace. He is realistic about the human plight. Humans are a radically fallen race among whom sin is ubiquitous. At the same time, Nouwen affirms that God is always going before God's people, drawing them to God's self, forgiving human rebellion and inviting them to return to the Father.[56] The poet-gardener builds on the hopefulness of this movement model of spiritual formation by affirming that life in God is a circuitous journey. To love God is not to be pathologically obsessed with religious habits but to keep in step with the Spirit who loves us perfectly.

Biblical Context: Preaching in Parables

"With many similar parables Jesus spoke the word to them, as much as they could understand. He did not say anything to them without using a parable. But when he was alone with his own disciples, he explained everything" (Mark 4:33, 34). Jesus' manner of public ministry is the touchstone of preaching for the poet-gardener. His preaching to the crowds avoided didactic, direct, hortatory methods. Instead, he opted for an indirect, imaginative way of communicating the Word. In surprising ways, the parables of Jesus remain among the most memorable and best loved stories in literature.

Why did Jesus choose this method of preaching? Mark characterizes Jesus' preaching as parabolic without comment as to his motives. Bible commentators have offered a variety of explanations. A number of scholars, drawing most notably on the work of William Wrede, theorize about a messianic secrecy motif in Mark as a partial explanation for Jesus' parabolic preaching. This theory postulates that Mark employs a secrecy motif as a literary and apologetic device to cover up suspicions about Jesus'

---

[56]Henri Nouwen, *Return of the Prodigal Son* (New York: Image Books, 1996), 98-109.

messianic identity. In this vein, Wrede suggests that Jesus' preaching was intentionally obtuse to create an aura of mystery around Jesus.[57]

Ben Witherington III contests messianic secrecy motifs in Jesus' methods of preaching. As an alternative, he suggests that Jesus' primary mode of preaching was wisdom speech characterized by an inherently veiled metaphorical approach.[58] Witherington asserts that Jesus' preaching was not secret keeping, but rather, "grounded in Jesus' own self-presentation as revealed indirectly by his chosen form of discourse and actions."[59] In keeping with his prophetic role and the apocalyptic tone of the gospel, Jesus spoke in ways that fulfilled Isaiah's prophecy of deafness and misunderstanding (Isaiah 6:9, 10). Jesus repeatedly urged, "If anyone has ears to hear, let him hear" (Mark 4:23). And yet, the earmark of wisdom speech is the absence of protracted explanations to ensure understanding. God alone gives spiritual ears to hear spiritual messages.[60]

The poet-gardener embraces Jesus' style of preaching in parables as a powerful way to deeply influence the consciousness of others. Rather than assuming that Jesus was attempting in some manner to keep people in the dark, the preacher hears Jesus' urgent words, "If anyone has ears to hear, let him hear," as an invitation to life transformation through the Word of God. What are some elements of parables that inform the poet-gardener approach to preaching?

---

[57] William Wrede, *The Messianic Secret,* trans. J.C. Grieg (Cambridge: James Clarke and Company, 1971).

[62] Ben Witherington, III, *The Gospel of Mark: A Socio-Rhetorical Commentary* (Grand Rapids, MI: Eerdmans, 2001), 42.

[63] Ibid., 41.

[64] Ibid.

John Bonsignor contributes to this discussion from the unlikely venue of legal education. In seeking ways to build a combination of analytical and reflective skills in law students, Bonsignor began to employ parables from a variety of sources, including Biblical sources. To his surprise, he found that students not only struggled with the parables and remembered them, but also showed a remarkably increased ability for rumination about legal questions. What Bonsignor discovered was that the form of communication is of equal importance to the content one seeks to communicate.[61]

Among modern thinkers, few have contributed more to careful analysis of spiritual communication than Soren Kierkegaard. In his reflections on parables, Kierkegaard wrote:

"An illusion (that a person is a Christian) can never be destroyed directly; only by indirect means can it be radically removed ... One must approach from behind the person who is under an illusion. A direct attack only strengthens a person in his illusion, and at the same time embitters him ... the indirect method, which loving and serving the truth, arranges everything dialectically for the prospective captive and then shyly withdraws."[62]

Kierkegaard was convinced that many people in church, including theologians, were spiritually dead. He observed people making professions of Christian faith, going to church regularly, and listening to sermons. And yet, he saw an absence of fruit from these religious practices. In Kierkegaard's estimation, an alarming percentage of religious people lacked a substantial spiritual life marked by an intense relationship with God.[63]

Where spirituality is concerned, Kierkegaard proposed that the parable is the best method of communication. Parables are "set in motion" by the teacher, but acted upon by

---

[61] John J. Bonsignor, "In Parables: Teaching Through Parables," *Legal Studies Forum,* 12, no. 1, (1988): 1-15.
[62] Ibid., 25.
[63] Ibid., 22-31.

the hearer. The parable takes the listener inward rather than allowing him or her to remain focused on external, conscious matters.

At the same time, Kierkegaard eschewed objective learning as a means for spiritual growth. The goal of a person in the spiritual quest must be to become subjective, and to live in subjective truth. In Kierkegaard's view, objectivity works to reduce the individual to an actor on a world stage. Subjectivity enlarges the person in private but powerful ways.[64]

Thomas Oden builds on Kierkegaard's analysis as he delineates five crucial dynamics at work in parables: He suggests that parables are better suited for carrying the freight of value inquiry and spirituality than logical analysis or speculative philosophy. In counter-intuitive ways, the simplicity of parables pierces consciousness more readily than complex arguments.

The parable allows deep, relational communication between the narrator and the listener. The parable begins innocently in the form of an engaging story. Listeners are disarmed, unthreatened, and readily drawn into the plot. The congregation goes beyond hearing the parable to experiencing the story first-hand. Listeners are drawn in and encouraged to compare features of the story, especially identification with certain characters, to their own experience.

The parable involves indirect communication that provokes self-discovery. Direct communication is the mode of choice for communicating information. By contrast, a parable presents a paradoxical situation with moral questions and no answers. If the ethical knot is to be untied, listeners must do so by inward reflection and intentional

---

[64]Soren Kierkegaard, *Concluding Unscientific Postscript,* (Princeton, NJ: Princeton University Press, 1968), 11.

choice. Whereas direct communication creates observers and listeners, indirect communication creates participants and actors.

In some measure, to listen to a parable is to lose control of one's responses to the story. The parable carries those who hear inwardly into unchartered waters of the soul. Through parabolic, indirect communication, the preacher cultivates the capability in the faith community for reflection and self-awareness. Direct learning adds to a person's knowledge but does not necessarily enhance the capability of the person. Indirect communication has the power to reframe consciousness, jolting the person out of previous mental routines. In keeping with the parable of the sower and the seed (Luke 8:4-8), the parable does not always fall on receptive ground. Nonetheless, the listener becomes aware in incipient ways that a world exists beyond his or her routine understanding.

Parables are memorable and amenable to oral tradition. As impactful as Jesus' parables are in written form, Oden suggests that their maximum efficacy lies in the nature of orality. These stories rehearse common, everyday scenarios with uncommon, unexpected twists. Moreover, parables leave the hearer with a question mark, a niggling "thorn in the mind" (per the 1999 film, *The Matrix*) that drives continued reflection well beyond the moment of storytelling.[65] These elements of paradox and question combine with the personal resonance of parables to create long-term memorability.[66]

A Parable for Preaching: The Sower and the Seed

---

[65] *The Matrix,* directed by Andy Wachowski and Larry Wachowski, Groucho II Productions, 1999.

[66] Soren Kierkegaard, and Thomas C. Oden, *Parables of Kierkegaard Kierkegaard's Writings* (Princeton, NJ: Princeton University Press, 1978), vii-xxi.

The crowds that followed Jesus acknowledged the uniqueness of his teaching: "When Jesus had finished saying these things, the crowds were amazed at his teaching, because he taught as one who had authority and not as their teachers of the law" (Matthew 7:28, 29). This reaction is full of irony. The teachers of the law strung together carefully developed, sophisticated morality teaching based upon detailed study of the Scriptures and Mishnah. By contrast, Jesus told simple stories that drew upon common, everyday events. Despite their seeming simplicity, Jesus' teaching was perceived as authoritative. Mark goes a step further to describe the words of Jesus as, "a new teaching" (Mark 1:27).

The newness and authority of Jesus' preaching arises from the incarnational intersection he brings between the Word of God and the consciousness of the hearer. As Jesus preaches about everyday life, he invites his listeners to detect the presence of God in mundane details. Like Elijah in the cave, those who are seeking to hear from God must listen for "a still small voice" (1 Kings 19:12).[67]

The parable of the sower and the seed (Luke 8:4-8) illustrates Jesus' indirect manner of preaching. There is nothing surprising or new in his observations about farming practices: "A farmer went out to sow his seed" (Luke 8:4). In that agrarian culture, everyone had some experience farming or watching farmers. The story line was so familiar that any of them could have told it. To sow, farmers took a handful of seed and broadcast it, throwing it in an arc. Imprecision was the order of the day: the better the

---

[67] Charles Cosgrove, W. Dow Edgerton, and Don Wardlaw, *In Other Words: Incarnational Translation For Preaching* (Grand Rapids, MI: Eerdmans, 2007), 115-116.

farmer, the better his aim. But even the best of farmers has some seed fall in places that do not grow well-footpaths, weedy patches, rocky soil.[68]

In a sense, the only surprise in this parable is Jesus' implication that it carries an important spiritual message. His story invites the listener to ponder about sowing seed and the fact that only some of the seed grows. Everyone knows Jesus is a carpenter, not a farmer. This is not a lesson in better farming practices. Rather, Jesus is urging folks to ask: "What is the rest of the story?" Note that he does not exhort the people to action with the single exception of an urgent invitation to hear. Truth is present in the parable but Jesus leaves it to the listener to discover it.

What are elements of the parable of the sower and the seed that inform the poet-gardener? Employing Thomas Oden's analytical map, several dynamics emerge in this parable. First, the story creates a subjective experience as the context for discovering the objective truth. The objective facts of farming are not in dispute. However, those who hear the story find themselves engaged at a deeper level of consciousness beyond the obvious. The subjective question is, "What does this story have to do with me?"

Jesus' indirect communication sets the stage for inquiry about spiritual matters. He avoids direct confrontation about the spiritual state of listeners. The people are listening to an entertaining, harmless story for the sheer enjoyment of listening to it. The fact that the parable carries significant spiritual import comes later.

The paradoxical quality of the parable gives it staying power in the memory. It remains as an unsolved mystery in the minds of listeners. And, the parable is both

---

[68] William Barclay, *The Gospel of St. Luke,* Daily Study Bible Series (Louisville: Westminster John Knox, 2001), 211.

personal and portable. It is a well-told story that listeners can appreciate and repeat to their friends.

Actually, the parable is intended not only to be heard but also to be repeated. Here is a primary mode through which parables work change: ongoing rumination and recounting of the story. Jesus is preaching for change, but not sudden, startling change. His metaphors of seed and soil point to the reality of what he has created in the heart of the listener, a growth process that will unfold over time and under proper conditions.

The parable of the sower and the seed is particularly germane to the poet-gardener model of preaching in its focus on issues of nurture and spiritual growth. Three out of four seeds fall in soil conditions that do not produce fruit. If it were not for the bountiful fecundity of the good soil, "a hundred times more than was sown" (Luke 8:8), the farmer would be bankrupt.[69]

The spiritual implications of the parable are yet more sobering. In Luke 8:11-15, Jesus interprets the parable for his disciples. What are some key implications for the spiritual life?

The seed is the Word of God. Jesus does not elaborate on the import of this statement, but at least one fact is evident. The Word of God is perfect and without flaw (Proverbs 30:5). An absence of fruit cannot be blamed on bad seed.

The fact that the Word of God is not heard and hence bears no fruit in some lives is in fulfillment of the prophecy given through Isaiah: "Though seeing, they may not see; though hearing, they may not understand" (Isaiah 6:9, 10). So, hearing God's Word is not

---

[69] Joseph A. Fitzmeyer, *The Gospel According to Luke I-IX,* vol. 28 of the Anchor Bible (New York: Doubleday, 1981), 366-368.

the same thing as believing. As a matter of fact, spiritual forces actively oppose human response to God.

Spiritual growth requires rootedness, depth of faith. Those on the rock hear God's Word. In fact, they respond enthusiastically with joy. But the Word of God is not insurance against the perils of life. When inevitable trials and temptations come to those with a surface relationship with God, their meager roots cannot hold against the storm.

The seed that fell among the thorns faces the challenge of daily living as a disciple in a fallen world. Jesus is never idealistic in his presentation of faith. Those who follow him continue to face a daily grind of worrisome circumstances and material distractions. In Jesus' estimation, the pressure of daily living can choke the spiritual life out of a person.

Fruitful soil for the Word of God is a person with "a noble and good heart" (Luke 8:15). Luke's version of the parable uniquely underlines the importance of "perseverance" in producing a crop. Again, fruit does not appear automatically or overnight. To be fruitful requires the right growth climate and a proper growing season.[70]

The poet-gardener understands that fostering fruitfulness in the lives of disciples is the point of preaching. More precisely, effective preaching is a vital part of creating a spiritual climate in which people can thrive and become fruitful. The proclaimed Word promotes the Biblical pattern of spiritual transformation in the form of core change within a faith community.

Seeds cannot plant or nurture themselves. If they are to grow to maturity, they require a gardener. In the same way, individuals cannot nurture their own spiritual vitality in the absence of a community. The parable of the sower and the seed is an urgent

---

[70] Joseph A. Fitzmeyer, *The Gospel According to Luke I-IX*, 366-368.

message to the faith community to tend the soil with an eye to ameliorating anti-growth conditions that are choking the spiritual life out of people.

In *Life Together,* Dietrich Bonhoeffer describes Christian community as both a necessity and a blessing from God. On the subject of Christian nurture he comments:

> "Christianity means community through Jesus Christ and in Jesus Christ. No Christian community is more or less than this. Whether it be a brief single encounter or the daily fellowship of years, Christian community is only this. We belong to one another only through and in Jesus Christ. What does this mean? It means, first, that a Christian needs others because of Jesus Christ. It means, second, that a Christian comes to others only through Jesus Christ. It means, third, that in Jesus Christ we have been chosen from eternity, accepted in time, and united for eternity."[71]

Bonhoeffer's premise is straightforward. Taking part in a "visible" Body of Christ is a great privilege, but it is also a necessary context of spiritual growth. The notion of individualistic faith violates a basic Biblical assumption. That is, Christian faith is grounded in the fundamental category of covenantal community.[72]

Theological Context: Relational Theology

In making a case for a relational theology of preaching, Alling and Schlafer assert: "Good preaching does not simply issue reports about God's sacred conversations. Rather good preaching engages listeners as additional partners in an already on-going 'Spirited' dialogue."[73] In other words, preaching that produces faith is always a shared work of the faith community.

Lori Carrell weighs in the conversation from the perspective of communication studies. She asserts that communication is "the process of individuals together co-

---

[71] Dietrich Bonhoeffer, *Life Together* (New York: HarperOne, 1978), 21.
[72] Ibid.,25.
[73] Roger Alling and David J. Schlafer, *Preaching as the Art of Sacred Conversations: Sermons That Work* (Harrisburg, PA: Morehouse, 1997), 11.

creating meaning; the process of connection."[74] In this vein, Carrell suggests the most valid locus for measuring the impact of preaching is the ear of the listener. She commends a process of listening as the metric for sermons, that is, preachers listening to listeners in order to determine if sermons worked. Such a view of communication comes against notions of preaching as a rhetorical monologue in which the attention of the preacher focuses on her or his words and presentation to the exclusion of attentiveness to the congregation's response.[75]

These valuable insights from communication studies reinforce the value of a relational theology of preaching. Cooper and McClure propose a theological typology for preaching that includes four predominant modes: Transcendent, relational, existential, and ethical-political.[76] In characterizing relational theology they suggest several distinctives.

In relational theology, the starting point is belonging. Humans have an inherent need to belong. The good news of the Gospel is that people belong to God and the Christian community. God's fundamental connectedness to all life, known most intimately in the imago Dei, is the foundation of Christian faith.

Relational theology emphasizes a view of sin as a social phenomenon, the fracturing of relationship with God and others. To live in sin involves twin deceptions. On the one hand, one denies that he or she belongs to God and to a community. On the other hand, sin compels one to assert a false sense of autonomy while remaining trapped in isolation.

---

[74] Lori Carrell, *The Great American Sermon Survey*, 33.
[75] Lori Carrell, *The Great American Sermon Survey*, 33.
[76] Byron Cooper and John McClure, *Claiming Theology in the Pulpit*. 10.

Relationship is an ontological reality, not a choice. To be a person is to be in relationship. One has and needs an individual identity, but that identity is not self-created. Personal identity grows out of community roots. Who I am is framed by my social milieu.

As much as one's persona is socially grounded, it is not a static reality. Rather, we live in process, constantly evolving or devolving in our interchange with those around us. The faith community is a context of possibilities in which we are becoming more fully human. Cooper and McClure assert that the Church is rightly seen as "The mother of our faith."[77]

An authentically Christian relational theology goes beyond warm and fuzzy notions of life together to affirm that relationship is grounded in suffering. We have a relationship with God through Christ's suffering on the cross. Equally, to love one another is to "lay down our lives for our friends" (John 15:13).[78]

Cooper's and McClure's typology further characterizes theology of preaching in terms of three presuppositions: The preacher's understanding of authority, worldview assumptions, and doctrinal distinctives.[79] When fleshing out a relational theology for the poet-gardener model, this typology suggests that the preacher holds views in each of these categories that under gird a relational trajectory. For the poet-gardener, authority and doctrine grow out of a worldview where connectedness to God and others are the fundamental, life giving realities of human experience.

What is the nature of authority to preach for the poet-gardener? Drawing upon the Wesleyan Quadrilateral, an analysis of authority might be couched in terms of four

---

[77] Byron Cooper and John McClure, *Claiming Theology in the Pulpit*. 10.
[78] Ibid., 17-19.
[79] Ibid., 140.

component dynamics: Authority of Scripture, authority of tradition, authority of experience, and authority of reason.[80] In regard to scriptural authority, Christian theology accommodates four predominant ways of understanding that might be labeled verbal inspiration, unique revelation, universal principles, and fresh address.[81]

The poet-gardener model builds upon the notion that God's Word is a fresh address to the preacher and the congregation. This interpretation assumes that the Bible contains a living Word of God that organically generates timely, multiple interpretations. These many interpretations are not mutually exclusive. Rather, the faith community receives the gift of God's collective wisdom that is both ancient and contemporary. As the poet-gardener preaches, he or she brings both God's past Word and inspiration to hear God's present Word. The poet-gardener affirms the truth found in 2 Timothy 3:16: "All of Scripture is God-breathed and is useful for teaching, rebuking, correcting, and training in righteousness."

Notwithstanding the ancient nature of the Scriptures, God uses any text in fresh and surprising ways to speak in a timeless way. The poet-gardener does not feel the need to pick and choose Bible verses that support his or her presuppositions. Instead, he or she assumes that God uses the Scripture to interrogate our lives and understanding. The preacher supports an on-going dialogue between the Church and God's Word, between revelation and interpretation.[82]

Cooper and McClure analyze authority of tradition under three rubrics: limited absoluteness, limited relativity, and absolute relativity. The poet-gardener views church

---

[80] John Wesley and Albert C. Outler, *John Wesley,* Library of Protestant Thought (New York: Oxford University Press), 71.
[81] Burton Cooper and John McClure, *Claiming Theology in the Pulpit,* 21-23.
[82] Ibid.

tradition as a living record of the work of the Holy Spirit. In God's wisdom, tradition is not a fixed, unbending set of rules, but rather a dynamic way of seeking to be obedient and faithful to God's Word. A mark of faithfulness is flexibility of the tradition to accommodate changes in the social context without dipping into thoughtless syncretism where core principles or beliefs are lost. Even more, changes in the social context may become a source of revelation of God's truth that previously had lain hidden in the shadows.[83]

How much authority can human experience have in informing Christian theology? The poet-gardener affirms a limited human capacity for experiencing spiritual reality on both public and private levels. At the same time, this model acknowledges human tendencies toward self-deception as well as the tendency for people to universalize their experience of God.

Drawing upon a theology that affirms the image of God within each person, the preacher trusts the ability of people to experience God in authentic ways. As Francis Bacon famously said, all human beings have the ability to read "God's second book, the book of God's works."[84] In this metaphorical language, Bacon points to God's general revelation that speaks to all people. Here is the basis for common human experience as a limited source of authority for preaching. While questioning the aphorism, "All paths lead to God," the poet-gardener can affirm that all spiritual paths begin with God and share a universal connection of longing for a fuller knowledge of the Creator.

Cooper's and McClure's typology of theology for preaching points to several ways of understanding the authority of reason. The poet-gardener affirms a way of

---

[83] Burton Cooper and John McClure, *Claiming Theology in the Pulpit,* 21-23.
[84] Francis Bacon and Michael Kiernan, *The Advancement of Learning,* Modern Library Science (New York: Random House, 2001), 3.

mutual transformation. Mutual transformation suggests that human reason operates with a dialectical tension. On the one hand, our reasoning is necessarily faulty-limited by finite capacity, self-deception, and subjectivity. On the other hand, God works much good, even transformation, through human reason. Jesus acknowledges the importance of reason: "Love the LORD your God with all your heart, and with all your soul, and with all your *mind*" (Matthew 22:37). (Italics added by the author.) In this quote, Jesus affirms that love of God is a holistic response of persons. Reason alone does not lead to faith. Rather, reason and faith interact in an ever deepening relationship with God.[85]

The poet-gardener preaches a message that is fundamentally counter-cultural and counter-intuitive. As such, the preacher acknowledges that people come to the faith community with a worldview shaped largely by cultural influences. To hear a Kingdom message requires reframing of these largely subconscious assumptions. In many ways, the poet-gardener works to commend an alternative meta-narrative that responds to the fundamental questions of life: Where did I come from? Why am I here? What is my purpose? Why is there evil in the world?

Left to our own devices, human beings develop a worldview from a combination of personal experience, folklore, and marketing campaigns. As an alternative, the poet-gardener offers a frame of reference that Cooper and McClure dub relational theism.[86] This meta-narrative portrays God as sustainer of life who loves humans in absolute freedom. There is a sense of give and take between God and God's created order. God has created each one of us with a vocation (Ephesians 2:10), but also with choices. In this vein, God is both immanent and transcendent. Charles Hartshorne characterizes God's

---

[85] Byron Cooper and John McClure, *Claiming Theology in the Pulpit*. 31.
[86] Ibid., 34.

relationship to the world: "The world is the body of God."[87] The world, including humans, is inextricably connected to the life of God. And yet, we have a life of our own. Behind every sermon lies a set of doctrinal beliefs that underpin the hermeneutical approach of the preacher.[88] The poet-gardener emphasizes relational categories across key doctrinal arenas. In questions related to theodicy, the poet-gardener responds to the problem of evil by underlining the paradoxical nature of God's sovereignty. On the one hand, God's power is unlimited. Although God could control all events and actions in the world to ensure that everything works perfectly, God expresses power in ways that go beyond control.

Ultimately, God's omni-powerful character is most revealed in love. And yet, God's love operates in an environment of freedom in which the created order may freely return God's love. Equally, people may choose alienation and rebellion from God.

A limited dominion understanding of theodicy does not minimize the reality of evil or the suffering that accompanies it. The poet-gardener affirms that God suffers alongside a suffering world, literally experiencing our pain. And, there is hope. Although existential angst is an undeniable reality, so are the promises of God. In the consummation of all things, God's grace and justice will prevail.

No theology of preaching is complete without a carefully reasoned theology of atonement. Specifically, what is the meaning of the cross? A relational theology of atonement builds on three key understandings. Sin equals alienation from God and others in which we become lost in our isolation and lack of belonging. Second, Christ's atoning

---

[87] Charles Hartshorne, *The Divine Relativity: A Social Conception of God,* The Terry Lecture Series (New Haven: Yale University Press, 1982), 11.
[88] Byron Cooper, and John McClure, *Claiming Theology in the Pulpit,* 39-41.

work is reconciliation between God and humanity and within the human community. Third, God's nature is Trinitarian, that is, fundamentally relational.[89]

The Johannine gospel interprets Jesus' atonement on the cross in terms of reconciliation and unity of God's people. In John 11:51ff. Caiaphas, the high priest, gives an unwitting prophecy about the nature and purpose of Jesus' death: "He prophesied that Jesus would die for the Jewish nation, and not only for that nation, but also for the scattered children of God, to bring them together and make them one." Raymond Brown points out that Jesus' prayer for unity echoes this relational theme for the atonement: "I pray that they may all be one as we are one. May they be brought to complete unity to let the world know that you sent me and have loved them" (John 17:20-23).[90] The next day, Jesus enacts the answer to his prayer on the cross.

A relational atonement theology points to God's priority on community. Although individual souls find salvation through Jesus' sacrificial death, individual salvation is not the only, nor even the primary, motive of the cross. In Jesus' crucifixion, God is renewing God's covenant with the people, a covenant sealed in blood. The life and death of Christ creates a new community, the Church, through the power of forgiveness and with the commission of reconciliation. The Church is not only a result of Christ's atonement. The Church is an eternal continuation of God's reconciling power at work in the world.

For the poet-gardener, the Church is fundamentally a missional community, charged with the responsibility to continue the reconciling work of Christ on earth. This understanding eschews any sense of arrogance over unbelievers. The Church stands in

---

[89] Ibid., 45-46.
[90] Raymond E. Brown, *The Gospel of John, I-XII,* vol. 29 of The *Anchor* Bible (New York: Bantam Doubleday, 1966), 319.

need of forgiveness and God's grace as much as all others. However, the Church is also a community filled with God's possibilities even as she depends on God's promises of redemption. Rather than seeing themselves as set apart from the world, the Christian community hears God's command to be ambassadors to a lost world: "All this is from God who reconciled us to himself through Christ and gave us the ministry of reconciliation: that God was reconciling the world to himself in Christ. And he has committed to us the message of reconciliation. We are therefore Christ's ambassadors" (2 Corinthians 5:18-20).

As a reconciling, transforming force in the world, the Church is called to meet people in the depth of their sin and fallen beliefs. There is no room for condemnation in these stark encounters. However, the preacher cannot afford to dismiss the need for forgiveness or the necessity of grace in making heart level changes. He or she relies upon the power of the Holy Spirit in using the preached word to change hearts and lives.[91]

The poet-gardener builds on a present-focused theology, but with the constant awareness of a dialectical tension between the temporal and the eternal. Drawing upon Jesus' promises of his return and the consummation of all things, the preacher acknowledges that God's Kingdom is with us and ahead of us. What happens in history matters to God as well as to us, but the final outcomes of life include a note of mystery.

To live as a faith community is to live with this ambiguity. On the one hand, Jesus has granted great authority to the Church: "I will give you the keys to the kingdom of heaven; whatever you bind on earth will be bound in heaven, and whatever you loose on earth will be loosed in heaven" (Matthew 16:19). On the other hand, Jesus repeatedly reminds his disciples that we know not the day or the hour of his return and final reign.

---

[91] Byron Cooper and John McClure, *Claiming Theology in the Pulpit,* 54-55.

For the poet-gardener, eternal life is the present moment experience of God's love and presence with us (John 17:3). Eternal life is a relational reality, not reducible to categories such as going to heaven. The preacher relies on God's promise that nothing can separate us from the love of God (Romans 8:39). He or she affirms that Christian faith is a "via ignota," the way of not knowing. While affirming the resurrection from the dead, the poet-gardener is also realistic about our limited human experience and knowledge. Human understanding is finite, unable to offer anything beyond what God has revealed about the nature of spiritual life beyond the grave.[92]

Social Context: Postmodern Worldview

To reflect on postmodernism as the social context for the poet-gardener model requires a paradoxical approach. Postmodern worldview is the frame of reference for the twenty-first century. If the poet-gardener hopes to connect with postmodern people, he or she must understand their point of view. This connection requires a posture of pleasant inflexibility, a combination of genuine curiosity about postmodern worldview and firmness to maintain Christian core convictions.

In many ways, postmodernism defies description. Following a deconstructionist impulse, Jacques Derrida, Hans-Georg Gadamer, and a host of theologians who have built on their philosophical reflections write in a way that resists analysis and categorization. In a real sense, those who would seek to understand postmodernism must be willing to play with the ideas behind the worldview.

Actually, the metaphor that Derrida and Gadamer share in common is play. From different perspectives both philosophers point to postmodernity as an era in which an understanding of the world cannot be worked out in the classical sense. They propose that

---

[92] Byron Cooper and John McClure, *Claiming Theology in the Pulpit,* 66-69.

modernity's fixed assumptions about certainty have been set aside in favor of a dynamic playing with experience and ideas.[93]

Jacques Derrida's playful definition of postmodern worldview emphasizes differences: "*Differance* is the systematic play of differences, of the traces of differences, of the spacing by means of which elements are related to each other."[94] This obscure statement is better understood in light of Derrida's precise use of language. "Difference" refers to spatial separation. Language used in one setting has different meaning than the identical language used in another setting. Alternatively, he uses "differance" to mean something closer to deference, or temporal separation among words. For Derrida, language used at one time means something different than the words spoken at another time.[95] In both cases, he is offering an alternative to the modern quest for certainty in the form of absolute final definitions. Derrida asserts that certainty is a myth. The only absolute is the absolute of play or interplay among competing ideas and experiences.[96]

By contrast, Hans-Georg Gadamer speaks of dynamics of play as *being played* by one's encounter with a text. He envisions truth as the experience one has in being subject to a text and its tradition rather than being the subject of one's own experience. He elaborates in the language of play:

> "When we understand a text, what is meaningful in it captivates us just as the beautiful captivates us. It has asserted itself and captivated us before we can come to ourselves and be in a position to test the claim to meaning that it makes. What we encounter in the experience of the beautiful and in understanding the meaning of tradition really has something of the truth of play about it. In understanding, we

---

[93] Jeffrey F. Bullock, "Preaching in a Postmodern Wor(l)d: Gadamer's Philosophical Hermeneutics as Homiletical Conversation," Christian Theological Research Group, http:// www.apu.edu/-CTRF/papers/1997, 1-7, (accessed date April 6, 2004).
[94] Jacques Derrida and Alan Bass, *Positions* (Chicago: University of Chicago Press,1981), 12.
[95] Robert Kysar and Joseph Webb, *Preaching to Postmodern: New Perspectives for Proclaiming the Message* (Peabody, MA: Hendrickson, 2006), 158-159.
[96] Jeffrey Bullock, "Preaching in a Post-Modern Wor(l)d," 3.

are drawn into an event of truth and arrive, as it were, too late, if we want to know what we are supposed to believe."[97]

The poet-gardener draws on Hans-Georg Gadamer's definition of experience or "Erfahrung," that is, an encounter with something or someone that asserts itself as truth.[98] For Gadamer, truth may not be equated with my subjective experience. Equally, he rejects the notion of empirically determine truth labeled as certainty per the scientific method. Rather, the "Erfahrung" suggests that truth is located in the open space of listening, questioning, and conversation.[99] In keeping with this postmodern view, preaching might be cast as a conversational "discipline that guarantees truth."[100] That is to say that the Word of God comes to us as a timeless communication from God discovered in the process of conversational interaction.

In describing their experience of Jesus' words, the two men who met him on the resurrected LORD on the road to Emmaus commented: "Were not our hearts burning within us while he talked with us on the road and opened the Scriptures to us?" (Luke 24:32). This story details a life changing experience with Christ, more specifically, with the Word of God, through the medium of a conversation among friends. Jeffrey Bullock suggests that this text captures the essence of preaching from a postmodern worldview in which conversational experience trumps logical argument and analysis.[101]

In analyzing shifts in postmodern thinking, Jeffrey Bullock points to a move away from the longstanding Aristotelian theories of rhetoric that emphasize the persuasive power of logic through symbolic language. Aristotle is famously quoted as saying:

---

[97]Hans-Georg Gadamer et al., *Truth and Method.*(London: Continuum Publishers, 2004), 102-110.
[98] Hans-Georg Gadamer et al., *Truth and Method,* 102-110.
[99] Jeffrey F. Bullock, "Preaching in a Postmodern Wor(l)d," 4.
[100] Gadamer, *Truth and Method,* 491.
[101] Bullock, 4.

"Spoken words are symbols of mental experiences and written words are the symbols for spoken words."[102] By contrast, the poet-gardener works with the postmodern ontological notion that experience and language are inseparable. Language creates experience and experience creates language.

Drawing upon the concepts of Lucy Rose, the poet-gardener envisions the preacher as a conversational partner with God and the congregation. Biblical texts are communications to be heard and answered before they are objects to be studied. Likewise, the preacher is in on-going conversation with the congregation in the shared experience of God's Word. As conversational partner, she or he listens and speaks as one among equals. The notion of partnership further implies that a message from God is never simply an individual, private message. The community's collective experience of God is the fullest expression of the living Word.[103]

Rose proposes conversational preaching as a challenge to traditional homiletical practice that relies on argument and representational language. She describes preaching as: "A time to gather the community of faith around the Word where the central conversations of the Church are refocused and fostered."[104] Noting that postmodern people place high value on individual experience, she suggests that our "small stories" become the starting points for preaching. In her view, sermons stretch out our lived experience toward the Word, engaging God and each other in a conversation about the meaning of our experiences in the light of God's Word.

---

[102] E.M. Edghill, trans., "De Interpretatione," 16a, in *The Basic Works of Aristotle,* ed. R. McKeon (New York: Random House, 1941), 40.
[103] Lucy Atkinson Rose, *Sharing the Word: Preaching in the Roundtable Church,* 8.
[104] Ibid.

The poet-gardener embraces heuristic starting points while seeking to avoid a radical subjectivism in preaching. Contrary to Rose's assertion that the only objective truth is eschatological, the poet-gardener affirms truth in the here and now. From a Biblical perspective, this position is an affirmation of the unity of the Word of God with the personality of Jesus. In the incarnational moment of preaching, the Word becomes flesh and dwells among us (John 1:14) and we experience the presence of the resurrected LORD who is the way, the truth, and the life.

Is there a connecting point between the incarnate presence of Christ and the deconstructed worldview of postmodern people? The poet-gardener employs the concept of "new consciousness" as an important cultural intersection. Derrida used the term "new consciousness" to characterize the goal of deconstruction. In this concept, he seeks to articulate the postmodern impulse to be an intellectual and spiritual energy that generates new understanding of ourselves as well as the world around us. He offers three categories for new consciousness. In speaking of word-consciousness, Derrida points to the wealth of meanings in a given word. Words do not have a single meaning. Rather, they have multiple meanings from historical and present contexts, including a hierarchy of meanings.

Secondly, Derrida characterizes human consciousness in terms of "trace." Our experiences and social interactions are fleeting, like a mist. In the same way, words have a reality, but they come and go quickly leaving only a trace. And yet, these traces are the building blocks of our lives as they connect past and present, conscious and unconscious, hopes and future.

And, Derrida coins the term, "spacing," to emphasize the importance of flow dynamics in consciousness. He speaks of flow as alternative to modernity's obsession with certitude by way of fixed categories. Derrida notes that the spaces in life, the pause between experiences and insights, are powerful realities. He uses the concept of spacing to point to the otherness of every experience. Our experiences are unique realities even though they contain traces of the past.[105]

The postmodern concept of new consciousness is not a new invention. Rather, the poet-gardener sees a connection with the ubiquitous Biblical theme of new creation. "Therefore, if anyone is in Christ, he is a new creation: the old has gone, the new has come!" (2 Corinthians 5:17). Here is a vital connecting point between Scriptural Christianity and the postmodern worldview. What postmodern philosophers characterize as the essential nature of human consciousness, the Gospel announces as a reunion with God in Christ-new consciousness that transforms human life.

With this philosophical and theological background in mind, how would one characterize the broader milieu of postmodernism in which the poet-gardener proclaims the Word? It is not likely that the average congregant can quote Foucault or has read extensively in Derrida. But, postmodern worldview is just that-a ubiquitous set of pre-conscious assumptions that affect the way that twenty-first century people make meaning out of their lives.

A summary of important characteristics of postmodern context might include at least four categories: authority issues, the locus of truth, centrality of experience, and yearning for community. John Francois Lyotard offers a summative statement about postmodernism that involves all of these elements: "Simplifying to the extreme, I define

---

[105] Robert Kysar and Joseph Webb, *Preaching to Postmoderns,* 153-158.

postmodern as incredulity toward meta-narratives."[106] The poet-gardener recognizes that he or she preaches to a generation of people who suffer from some degree of spiritual, moral, and intellectual homelessness. The unquestioned "big story" that once provided a framework for meaning has been rejected as a bed rock of authority, leaving a vacuum.

In commenting on the shift away from traditional meta-narrative, Graham Cole suggests that postmodern people operate from a perspectival approach in which truth depends on your perspective.[107] In this mindset, authority arises not so much from the question, "What is true?" as the functional question, "What will work?" Postmodernism promotes a hermeneutic of suspicion that questions the legitimacy of authority as a first impulse until proven otherwise.[108]

In a sense, the authority of the preacher and the authenticity of the person meld into a single category for postmodern listeners. Small, personal stories trump the big story, but only if the perception of the personal stories is that they are genuine. The poet-gardener model affirms that the personal testimony of the preacher is a significant source of authority in a postmodern context.

Moreover, the postmodern perspectives on truth and experience are two pieces of a whole. Experience, one's own experience, is the primary locus of truth. Graham Cole recalls an incident in which he was sharing his faith with a young adult who responded, "I'm happy for you, but my experience is different."[109] A pluralistic worldview is foundational for postmoderns.

---

[106] Jean Francois Lyotard, *The Postmodern Condition: A Report on Knowledge,* vol. 10, Theory and History of Literature (Minneapolis: University of Minnesota Press, 1984), xxiv-xxv.

112 Graham Cole, "Preaching Christ in a Postmodern World," *Perspective* vol. 8, no. 1, 2000, http://www.perspective.org.au, (accessed date August 6, 2008).

113 Ibid.

114 Ibid.

Whereas modern thinking relies upon reason, and especially, empirical evidence, as the primary source of truth, postmodern people are self-referential. The truth is my truth which is probably different from your truth. This worldview rejects the hegemony of reason over human consciousness. Equally, postmoderns view truth claims on the basis of revelation with a deep skepticism, that is, unless they themselves have seen an angel.

How might the poet-gardener preach in a climate characterized by self-referential subjectivism and the relative view of truth that follows? He or she understands that twenty-first century people thirst for a combination of personal connection and boldness of belief. As a generation swimming in clever marketing appeals, postmodern people have long antennae for manipulation. They are seeking to know the preacher's own true story which might connect with their own experience. Before listeners can believe what the preacher is saying, they must believe who the preacher is. The poet-gardener sees the importance of apologetics, but more as a witness of "This I believe" than logical, propositional arguments for the faith.

In *Life of the Beloved: Spiritual Living in a Secular World,* Henri Nouwen suggests that the desire to belong is the first impulse of faith.[110] The poet-gardener model affirms that responding to a longing for community is an essential part of effective preaching. As a related notion, Robert Kysar and Joseph Webb suggest that "community meaning" is a basic category of the sermon that speaks to the shared quality of spiritual life.[111]

When the poet-gardener preaches, he or she holds a bundle of truth in each hand. In the one hand, she holds nuggets of truth gleaned from hours spent immersed in the

---

[110] Henri Nouwen, *Life of the Beloved,* 14-15.
[111] Robert Kysar and Joseph Webb, *Preaching to Postmoderns,* 209-210.

Word of God. In the other hand she holds her compassion for the needs and longings of the congregation. This tandem approach to preaching leads to a particularity of meaning and application of the Biblical text. In other words, the text has a fresh, particular meaning for these people gathered at this time.

Particularity is a defining quality of preaching for the poet-gardener. When preaching a Biblical text, he or she proclaims with a desire that it might mean something for a particular congregation under particular circumstances at a particular time in history.[112] And, this particularity cannot be reduced to clever tips for living a better life. The preacher is concerned about building community life. As the church is conformed to the image of Christ, truth will flow. This understanding comports with postmodern mentality that equates truth with the experience of authentic community.[113]

---

[112] Thomas Long, *The Witness of Preaching* (Louisville: Westminster John Knox), 1990, 77.
[113] Robert Kysar, Robert and Joseph Webb, *Preaching to Postmoderns,* 208.

Source: Don Stephens, http://www.wordpress.com

MOVEMENT TWO: POETIC AND IMAGINATIVE ELEMENTS IN PREACHING

"Do I need to draw a picture for you?"

As one of seven children, I grew up in a family that taxed my parents' resources in every way, including their time and patience. My father was a stern man who gave orders that he expected to be followed without question. He was especially exasperated when he had to repeat himself. I can still hear his strained tone as he would say, "Do I need to draw a picture for you to understand me?"

I never dared to respond to my father's rhetorical question, but the answer is "yes." Human communication is imagistic-a kaleidoscope of mental pictures- at the most primary level. Researchers in communication universally agree that humans build language and make sense of the world through pictures, symbols, and metaphors that connect the unfamiliar with the familiar, the imaginative with memory. Mary Warnock describes human imagination in terms of a "seeing as" capacity that "mediates between the world and the self in a way that opens the self to the world."[114]

The poet-gardener intentionally employs imaginative theology in preaching. The preacher's job is to draw a picture, or more accurately, create an image that might serve as a medium for God's revelation. In contrast to models of preaching that cast sermons as logical arguments, the poet-gardener emphasizes the essential role of imagination in preaching. And yet, care must be exercised to avoid conceptual pitfalls regarding the nature and efficacy of human imagination. The poet-gardener model is not an exaltation of human ingenuity and creativity, but rather an exploration of ways we might faithfully encounter God holistically, including through the engagement of human imagination.

The Scriptures display deep suspicion about the nature of human imagination. In the prelude to the account of the Flood, the writer of Genesis comments about the state of

---

[114]Mary Warnock, *Imagination* (Berkeley: University of California Press, 1976), 194.

human affairs: "The LORD saw that the wickedness of man was great in the earth, and that every *imagination* of the thoughts of his heart was only evil continually. And the LORD was sorry that he had made man on the earth, and it grieved him to his heart" (Genesis 6:5, 6, RSV). Following the Flood, God covenants with all of creation to never again curse the earth because of human wickedness. Even so, this promise from the lips of God is tempered with realism about the fractious nature of human beings, particularly human imagination, "For the *imagination* of man's heart is evil from his youth" (Genesis 8:21, RSV). Later in the history of Israel, the prophet Isaiah warns against the rebellious quality of imagination. "All day long I have held out my hands to an obstinate people, who walk in ways not good, pursuing their own *imaginations*" (Isaiah 65:2). (Italics in Biblical references have been added by the author.) From a Biblical perspective, human imagination is an ambiguous ability used for ill as often as it is used for good.

The importance of imagination was further called into question under the influence of Greek philosophy, particularly Aristotelian notions of rhetoric. In classical rhetorical theory, metaphors and images were relegated to "pathos," (passion) a corollary function to ethos (core message) and kineo (persuasiveness). In rhetoric, metaphors and images were utilized as figures of speech that serve a non-essential, ornamental supporting role to logical argument.

Medieval thinking operated with similar metaphysical presuppositions. As such, imagination came to be conceptualized as imitation of the real, lacking any substance in its own right. As Edward Murray observes, imagination became mimetic, "the equivalent of imitating or copying through the construction of an object that resembled the model."[115]

With the dawn of the Enlightenment, theologians began to embrace dualistic presuppositions in which "real" equated with empirical observation and "imaginative" came to mean fanciful. In the modern era, the concept of imaginative theology became an oxymoron. Historical biblical criticism exerted its hegemony as the only legitimate pathway to understanding and proclaiming the Word of God.

Richard Eslinger characterizes modern preaching as suffering from "methodological schizophrenia." He suggests that predominant models of preaching reflect a collision of rationalistic and romantic notions of communication. On the one hand, rational approaches seek to discover the kernel of truth in the Scripture through quasi-scientific dissection of the text. On the other hand, the preacher seeks to build lively, memorable sermons that connect with people. To connect with listeners without losing connection with the text, modern preachers turn to historical imagination, an effort to recreate the setting and lived reality of the original context. The final ingredient in the modern sermon recipe is the use of gripping, vivid stories that illustrate the fallen condition in the historical context as a contemporary dilemma, too. Eslinger describes this mix of approaches in modern sermons as "rationalistic points, propositions, and subthemes illustrated by emotive, pathos-laden anecdotes."[116]

Four Hermeneutical Assumptions

The poet-gardener seeks to go beyond the dualistic tug-o-war between rhetorical and imaginative categories that inhere in modern preaching. As an alternative, the poet-

---

[115] Edward Murray, "Imagination Theory and Phenomenological Thought" *Phenomenological Psychology*, ed. Edward L. Murray (Pittsburgh: Duquesne University Press, 1987), 133.

[116] Richard L. Eslinger, *The Web of Preaching* (Nashville: Abingdon, 2002), 248.

gardener preaches out of a hermeneutic of imaginative theology. This hermeneutic entails four assumptions:

1. Imagination serves as an alternative and legitimate paradigm for encountering God's revelation.
2. Images embody a unique language or grammar.
3. Imagination drives the volitional life and is a key element of motivation.
4. Imagination implies assumptions about epistemology.

Imagination: A Paradigm for Encountering God

"Human possibilities are limited by human imagination."[117]

The poet-gardener preaches to expand the possibilities in the lives of her or his listeners. With faith that human potential hinges on the experience of God's grace, the preacher seeks to communicate graceful alternatives to human engineered norms. This task requires an encounter with God that confronts the master images of culture which dictate what is proper and possible. The goal in preaching is not to be creative and clever, but to be faithful to God's vision for the world. By helping listeners open their human imagination in new ways, the preacher offers a glimpse of God's imagination for the world.

Various theologians have attempted to characterize divine imagination at work in human consciousness. Samuel Taylor Coleridge coined the term, "esemplastic," to point to the inspired imagination. He suggested that humans have a hard-wired esemplastic imagination to encounter the divine. Coleridge conceived of inspired or poetic imagination as a higher order, secondary function in contrast to primary imagination, the human process that translates sensory perception into memory and cognition. This second order imaginative capability operates as an integrating and assimilating function through

---

[117] Garrett Green, *Imagining God: Theology and the Religious Imagination* (San Francisco: Harper and Row, 1989), 83.

which humans shape a new understanding of the world where the perceptual fragments equal more than the whole.[118]

Garrett Green has proposed that imagination is much more than a human ability to encounter God. Rather, he suggests that imagination is God's venue for revelation, coining the term, "paradigmatic imagination," to express this theological concept. To understand the place of human imagination in theology, one must carefully distinguish between God's revelation and the "inner sight" of imagining. Clearly, Christian theology does not equate the two. Human imagination cannot create an authentic message from God. Rather, imagination serves as the locus for receiving God's revelation. "The specifically Christian content (of imagination) derives not from the fact that we imagine but rather from what it is we are imagining. Christian imagining, like all human imagining, is dependent on the paradigms that make it possible by giving it shape and substance. The theologically decisive point is not the imagination in the formal sense as a human ability but its concrete content."[119]

This focus on imaginative encounter with God does not compete with "truth communication," but rather suggests a different paradigm for truth. Instead of limiting truth to propositions and logical arguments, the poet-gardener understands God's truth as an alternative way of seeing reality. The human imagination plays a vital role here. As Green suggests, "Religions characteristically employ this power of imagination in order to make accessible the ultimate shape, the organizing pattern of reality itself, thereby illuminating the meaning and value of human life."[120]

---

[118] Samuel Taylor Coleridge, *Critical Theory since Plato* ed. Hazard Adams (New York: Harcourt Brace Janovich, 1971), 469-471.
[119] Garrett Green, *Imagining God,* 90.
[120] Ibid.

H. Richard Niebuhr summed up revelation in terms of images: "Revelation is that special occasion which provides us with an image by means of which all the occasions of personal and common life become intelligible."[121] In other words, revelation by necessity exceeds human logical constructs and presuppositions. It is only through God-given images that we begin to see beyond a human constructed world. In this sense, all theology is imaginative.

Imaginative theology works with an inherent tension between pathways of seeing and hearing as means through which humans receive God's revelation. On the one hand, paradigmatic imagination is a new way of seeing, "*See*, I am doing a new thing!" (Isaiah 43:19). On the other hand, hearing the Word of God is God's chosen pathway for touching the hearts of God's people. "Faith comes from *hearing* the message and the message is heard through the word of Christ" (Romans 10:17). The poet-gardener preaches with the conviction that hearing the Word of God enables us to imagine God, that is, to "see" God without "seeing" God.

Archetypal images embedded in the Scripture serve as primary intersections between human imagination and revelation. Drawing upon the work of Carl Jung, Philip Wheelwright suggests that such images represent archetypal imagination. He uses archetype to refer to meta-images that embody both cognitive and constitutive functions in human understanding. For Wheelwright, archetypes are images of universal scope, possessing qualities of shared meaning across generations and cultures.[122]

Archetypal images of God in the Scripture are legion: Father, Son, Holy Spirit, light, wind, Word, fire, cross. For the poet-gardener, a key function of preaching is to

---

[121] Richard H. Niebuhr, *The Meaning of Revelation* (New York: McMillan, 1941), 109.
[122] Phillip Wheelwright, *The Burning Fountain: A Study in the Language of Symbolism* (Bloomington, IN: Indiana University Press, 1968), 80.

discern precise ways that the content and power of these master images of God might intersect with the imaginations of postmodern people. Certainly, the preacher is concerned about intersection points in the inner life of listeners. Equally, the poet-gardener is conscious of the lived reality of the faith community. The poet-gardener is keenly aware that his or her listeners are bombarded by powerful cultural images that shape their thinking, worldview, and sense of what is possible. Preaching that breaks into the consciousness of listeners confronts dominant master images of secular culture with Biblical images of realty.

In fact, communities hear sermons through the filter of a secular hermeneutic that draws its substance in large part from images created by media and marketing campaigns. Often, a secular paradigm includes many presuppositions about the nature of God and humans that stand in direct opposition to a Biblical worldview.

In this context, spiritual transformation is a change of paradigms before it is a change of thinking. The poet-gardener preaches with the conviction that a redemptive relationship with God flows out of a restored image of God. The need for attention to distorted images of God is particularly acute in an era in which the majority of persons are marginally acquainted with the Bible. George Hunter has characterized the twenty-first century as an age of "ignosticism." With this term Hunter is suggesting that the dominant theological view in postmodernism is a vague theism in which belief is supported by a paucity of content from Scripture.[123] A primary soul care goal in preaching is the enhancement of listeners' ability to imagine God in ways that comport with God's self-revelation in the Scripture.

---

[123] George Hunter, III., *Church for the Unchurched* (Nashville: Abingdon, 1996), 92.

This brief discourse on paradigmatic imagination would be incomplete without some reflection on the nature of the imago Dei and implications of this theological truth for the poet-gardener model. Christian theologians have debated the nature of imago Dei for centuries. Metaphysical presuppositions dominated much of the debate, narrowing speculation to questions about the substantive qualities of imago Dei. Garrett Green has suggested that imago Dei might be more accurately characterized in relational and functional terms.[124] That is to say, Green asserts that imago Dei plainly means humans are like God in some, basic definitive way. We bear a family resemblance. But, the key of our divine likeness is not a "divine spark" as Greek mystery religions might suggest. The imago Dei might be more accurately understood as a pattern for life and relationships that humans model after God.

A functional definition of imago Dei raises the question: What does imago Dei empower human beings to do? In the Sistine Chapel, Michelangelo created an iconic image that speaks to this question. In his famous rendering of creation, Michelangelo envisions God giving life to Adam through a touch-straining forward to touch Adam's finger. This painting suggests that life begins when God touches life. The image of God is the God-given ability to touch or connect with God. Imagination about God, then, is not a fanciful flight of possibilities which are entirely subjective. Rather, to hold the image of God is to experience a connection, a touch of God's hand in our imaginations. Since we have the true image of God, we are enabled to imagine God rightly, to have real knowledge of God.

---

[124] Garrett Green, *Imagining God: Theology and the Religious Imagination*, 87.

Language and Grammar of Images

A young woman I observed in a jewelry store in Miami provided an especially poignant example of the language and grammar of images. She was shopping for earrings. After the clerk had shown her several selections, the young woman exclaimed, "I'm looking for cross earrings like the ones Madonna wears. You know, the ones with the naked man on them."

When I recovered from my shock at this irreverent statement, I began to reflect on the many ways that images speak to people. Images, even religious ones, hold a wide spectrum of meaning based on the interpretive schema of the observer. Perhaps no image speaks a wider range of language than the cross. In other words, images do not hold an inherent value that speaks in the same way to every person. As Martin Marty soberly commented, "The cross on the Crusaders' shields is 'other' than the one on which the cancer patient fixes in desperate and consoling prayer."[125]

The poet-gardener approaches the exegesis of images as a key task in preaching. No image is simply a given; an interrogation is in order before the image qualifies to carry freight in the sermon. The language is especially ambiguous in master images created by the mass media. Thomas Troeger suggests that these secular images contain an "implicit gospel" that promotes a personal identity founded on ownership, acquisition, and competition. To make matters worse, mass media images understand human communities as "markets" with the goal of attaining and holding market share.[126]

And yet, preaching that is comprehensible to postmodern listeners cannot solve the problem of contaminated images with an iconoclastic strategy that seeks to

---

[125] Martin Marty, "The Long Road to Reconciliation," *Newsweek* 27(March 2000), 61.
[126] Troeger, Thomas G. "Imaginative Theology: The Shape of Postmodern Homiletics," *Homiletic* 13, no.1, (1988), 31.

eliminate images, even those that offer false messages, from the conversation. Garrett Green observes that Christian theology has suffered historically from an iconoclastic bias that assumes the least metaphoric language of God is best.[127] Alternatively, the poet-gardener preaches with the understanding that all language of God is metaphorical. The key in faithful preaching is a delicate balance. Preachers must assiduously avoid the idolatrous impulse to create pictures which claim, "God *is* this." At the same time, effective sermons engage in critical theology that distinguishes between appropriate and inappropriate paradigms that assert God to be "*as* or *like*."

Ella Bozarth-Campbell contributes to the conversation with her observations about icons and the authentic contribution iconic images might make to Christian faith. She refutes the notion that icons are idols, graven images, meant to supplant God and be worshipped in their own right. Instead, she characterizes icons as "A meeting place with the divine. The icon's power resides not in its ability to imitate anything, but in its capacity to disclose the Word (logos) itself . . . The presence of the logos in the image constitutes the seat of its energy."[128]

Concerns about idolatrous lapses in Christian expression are always appropriate. The popular aphorism is true: "God created humans in God's own image and we have been trying to return the favor ever since." How might issues of language and grammar of images help in distinguishing between idolatry and faithful use of images of God? Idolatrous images make the claim to fully describe or even materially embody God. Idolatry says, "Here is your god." By contrast, "Christo-morphic"[129] images speak the

---

[127] Garrett Green, *Imagining God*, 95.
[128] Ella Bozarth-Campbell, *The Word's Body: An Incarnational Aesthetic of Interpretation* (Tuscaloosa, AL: Alabama University Press, 1979), 104.
[129] Garrett Green, *Imagining God*, 212.

language of witness or testimony. For example, John the Baptist offered a Christo-morphic image of a lamb in witnessing to Jesus the Messiah: "Behold, the Lamb of God who takes away the sin of the world!" (John 1:29). For Christians, the paradigm of God is Jesus Christ. Images are faithful to the extent that they point beyond themselves to Christ as "The image of the invisible God, the firstborn over all creation" (Colossians 1:15).

Imagination, Motivation, and the Volitional Life

The poet-gardener uses images in preaching for purposes of inspiration and motivation far beyond the ornamental, attention-grabbing categories implied by the term, "sermon illustrations." Sermons that are memorable and impactful not only offer paradigmatic images of the Kingdom of God. Rather, the entire sermon is intended to serve as a motivating master image.

Drawing upon the language of Walter Brueggemann, master images foster prophetic imagination as they offer an alternative future to the listener in view of God's activity in the world.[130] Drawing upon Biblical narratives, Walter Brueggemann has articulated a model of prophetic imagination for preaching that motivates persons to seek justice and righteousness. He equates the preacher with prophet as he writes: "It is the vocation of the prophet to keep on conjuring and proposing alternative futures to the single future that the king wants to urge as the only thinkable one."[131] He goes on to suggest that the task of prophetic ministry is to nurture, nourish, and evoke a consciousness and perception alternative to the consciousness and perception of the dominant culture around us. Prophetic imagination entails four primary movements:

1. Reappropriation of corporate memory of God's salvific actions in the past.
2. Criticism of the current unjust order that defies God's justice.

---

[130] Walter Brueggemann, *The Prophetic Imagination* (Philadelphia: Fortress, 1978), 13.
[131] Ibid., 45.

3. Energizing marginalized persons toward an alternative future.
4. Offering doxology to God for God's deliverance and salvation.¹³²

In a sense, prophetic imagination gives the poet-gardener the motivation to confront dominant secular images that claim to be authoritative while offering deformative priorities. Brueggemann suggests that postmodern listeners and the 21ˢᵗ century Church are enslaved to ubiquitous images from marketers: "The contemporary American church is so largely acculturated to the American ethos of consumerism that it has little power to believe or act."¹³³ The poet-gardener confronts this "managed reality" by evoking images of God at work doing a new thing.

Notice that the poet-gardener employs an imagistic sermonic movement in contrast to the standard pattern of argument or logical refutation. To employ logical points and sub-points in argument against a powerful image is a study in frustration. Images always trump abstract thoughts in human memory. One might conceive metaphorically of logical arguments as fishing with a cane pole, employing a single line and hook to catch the unwary fish. By contrast, images have many "hooks" or points of contact, more like the adhesive product, Velcro.¹³⁴

Confronting vivid, resilient secular images requires the sermon to offer alternative gospel images that have the same degree of "stickiness" in human memory. For example, sports images, particularly football, are enormously powerful in American marketing. Images of football heroics promote many positive values: strength, teamwork, courage, hard work. The problem, of course, is that these images entail many troubling messages as well: violence, self-centered pride, competition, and hero worship.

---

¹³² Walter Brueggemann, *The Prophetic Imagination*, 13.
¹³³ Ibid., 23.
¹³⁴ Dan Heath and Chip Heath, *Made To Stick: Why Some Ideas Survive and Others Die* (New York: Random House, 2007), 51.

Thoughtful sermons might offer football images as a point of contact with the prior assumptions of listeners and then proceed with an ironic dissection of the images that points out the down side of this American icon. A poet-gardener approach to preaching offers no argument to football icons. Instead, the preacher might work with the image in surprising, "what if" directions. What if we organized the KFL-the Kingdom Football League? What if the point of the game in the KFL was to promote God's values such as unity and cooperation? Wouldn't this change the point of the game? How many points would the average KFL football game have if every game began with a kickoff where the kicking team ran down the field and helped the receiving team move down the field as effortlessly as possible, even carrying the runner with the ball if he tired midway? Can we envision all the players of both teams rejoicing in the end zone for the shared victory of another touchdown? Such a drastically alternative use of a dominant image motivates the listener on her or his own to reexamine dominant messages that remain otherwise unchallenged.

In light of the hegemony of logical, linear methodology in sermons for the past three hundred years, it is an ironic fact that the Old Testament prophets and Jesus employed imaginative, poetic expression, not linear prose, to motivate the faith community toward repentance and transformation. Biblical prophets understood the distinctive power of imagistic language to evoke newness and used it prolifically in their writings. The common caricature of the prophets portrays them as sad sack naysayers wearing sandwich board signs, "Repent, the end is near."

This cartoonish image is partly correct. Prophets courageously proclaimed oracles, messages of doom that embodied the burden of guilt and punishment. Criticism of what is wrong in the existing order is a part of their message. But, criticism by itself is rarely motivating to anyone. As much as the prophets criticized, they also sought to motivate and energize the people of God to repentance. The energy for repentance comes from a renewed memory within the community of God's faithfulness in the past that points to the promise of God's faithfulness for the future. With the inspiration of the imaginative method of the prophets, the poet-gardener preaches with the conviction that humans need both conviction and hope.

After a recent visit to church, I asked my granddaughter what she had learned that morning. "It was just the same old thing," she replied. Here is the common complaint of churchgoers. Sermons are seen as predictable words that reinforce what we already know and experience. The expectation that God will do a new thing is very low.

How ironic! The Word of God claims about itself, "So is my word that goes out from my mouth: It will not return to me empty, but will accomplish what I desire and achieve the purpose for which I sent it" (Isaiah 55:11). Brueggemann suggests that God's energizing work in the faith community always faces our tendency to domesticate the Word and tame God. A primary way that the Church robs God's Word of its newness and fruitfulness is by reducing the Word to our words. God speaks a Word and things that were not come into being. Too often, sermons take the creative Word and translate it into a message of "the same old thing."

No one is energized by a constant refrain from the pulpit, "OK, now let's do the same thing one more time with feeling." The poet-gardener draws upon Brueggemann's insight that humans are energized by what is promised and anticipated, not what we already possess and control. At a subconscious level, faith communities are often co-opted by the belief that there will never be newness, only rearranging of the furniture, the moving of old pieces into different patterns.[135]

In many ways, the task of the poet-gardener is to break through the routinization and numbness of listeners to offer a taste of freedom. Imagination is a critical venue to foster freedom. After all, it is the inherent freedom of imagination that makes it both winsome and dangerous at the same time. Through an imaginative encounter with God, faith communities are able to catch a glimpse of the incongruities in their carefully managed lives. As much as Americans value rights to life, liberty, and the pursuit of happiness, the unspoken reality is that people must live within the boundaries set by the dominant culture.

The 1998 motion picture, *The Truman Show,* is a science fiction comedy that dramatizes the unconscious captivity and need for freedom that lie beneath the surface of every day experience. In the movie, Truman Burbank, the main character, spends his entire life unaware of the fact that he is the central character of a constructed reality soap opera. As a matter of fact, Truman is the only person in the town of Seaside who is not a cast member. Even his wife is an actress. He lives happily unaware of the managed reality of his life until a series of small scripting and staging errors cause him to wonder. Eventually, Truman sees the truth of his captivity. Ironically, he is unable to overcome his phobia of bridges to escape his island home and embrace freedom.[136]

What a parable of the existential dilemma of twenty-first century life this film portrays! As Truman experienced, dawning awareness of captivity to the values of

---

[135] Walter Brueggemann, *Prophetic Imagination,* 23.
[136] *The Truman Show,* directed by Peter Weir and Andrew Niccol Hollywood, Paramount Pictures, 1998.

dominant culture is important but not sufficient to transformation. Faith communities must have guidance in confronting crippling fears that hold people in the prescribed roles and situations of their lives. Here is the dual task of poet-gardener preaching: Empowering imagination to see how life might yet be under the reign of God and encouraging the faith community to step beyond their fears into the new found freedom of the LORD.

Brueggemann points to four critical movements of imaginative preaching that creates the possibility of freedom:

1. Employing evocative images and metaphors that are powerful enough to confront the angst in people's lives and break through the numbness that has become a habituated coping style.
2. Naming the fears and terrors that have been denied and suppressed so deeply that we don't know they are there. This "naming" is done most powerfully through images and metaphors, not analytical speech. As people find expression for their fears, they also come to own their shadow side, making it accessible to God for healing and redemption.
3. Giving permission for the faith community to grieve the many losses that remain unresolved and unspoken. In this movement, sermons resist the temptation to hurry over grief or gloss the suffering and anguish of people.
4. Pointing to the cross as the ultimate metaphor of imagination for God's character and faithfulness. The poet-gardener proclaims in the cross the death of an old consciousness and the birth of new life in Christ.[137]

Freedom and motivation go hand in glove. The poet-gardener confronts two major pathologies of twenty-first century life, denial and despair, by offering the faith community an imaginative glimpse of an alternative future through the power of redemption. An essential companion to motivation is a sense of knowing God in new ways-a rediscovered epistemology.

Imagination and epistemology

---

[137] Walter Brueggemann, *Prophetic Imagination,* 32.

"Keeping it real." This aphorism might well serve as a slogan for the twenty-first century Church. Preachers are acutely aware of the desire of listeners to hear sermons that are relevant, believable, and full of the grittiness of real life. In this vein, the poet-gardener's reliance upon imaginative theology in preaching seems counter-intuitive since imagination is often understood to major in illusion. Garrett Green suggests that modern assumptions about epistemology, and specifically, the role of imagination in knowing, are inadequate: "Imagination turns out to be not the opposite of reality, but rather the means by which manifold forms of both reality and illusion are mediated to us. Imagination designates the human locus of God's revelation."[138]

Here is a major premise of the poet-gardener model. The center of epistemology is revelation; ultimate truth is given by God, not discovered by human ingenuity. Preaching serves as a modality of revelation, a strategic moment in which God discloses details of God's character and activity in the world. In a sense, the starting question for the poet-gardener is always, "How is God making God's self accessible to us in this time and place?"

Many narrative preachers suggest that human stories are a major venue for knowing God. For these theologians, the Bible is more than a series of stories about God's encounter with humans. Eugene Peterson describes the Biblical narrative as the intersection of salvation history (Heilgeschichte) and soul history (Seelgeschichte).[139] The role of preaching is to point to the overlap between the meta-story of God's work in the world and the micro-story of individual lives. The Bible is full of stories of common

---

[138] Garrett Green, *Imagining God*, 84.
[139] Eugene Peterson, *Five Smooth Stones for Pastoral Work* (Grand Rapids, MI: Eerdmans, 1992), 84.

people living in ordinary circumstances-Ruth, Tamar, Bartimaeus, Eunice. The good news is that no person's soul story is inconsequential in God's eyes.

Through the imaginative lens of narrative theology, the poet-gardener creates sermons that embody a "narrative shape," that mirrors the lived reality of the listeners. Narrative shape is more than mere imitation or observation of the human condition. Rather, the supposition here is a God-given pattern for life and relationships that is as much a part of the divine plan as the design of the human body. Humans grow in knowledge and love of God by living into the story line that God has planned for them. To the extent that human beings have erred from the path of God's will, the consequence of sin is a loss of ability to imagine what God is like, what God has planned for human life, and who we are as human beings.[140]

Narrative frames of reference emphasize the relational dimensions of epistemology. Biblical stories build upon "knowing" persons, as in "Abraham *knew* Hagar and she was with child" (Genesis 16:4, KJV). In a sense, the original sin, eating from the tree of knowledge of good and evil, was a fracturing of God's intent for the way humans were meant to know.

In the beginning, to know God was to be in intimate relationship with God, the source of all knowledge. The temptation to eat from the tree of knowledge of good and evil was an attempt to become knowledgeable by other means, circumventing relationship and going straight to the facts. Like the character, Jack Webb, from the old detective show, *Dragnet,* humans have been seduced ever since into equating facts with knowledge: "I just want the facts, Ma'am, just the facts."

---

[140] Eugene Peterson, *Five Smooth Stones for Pastoral Work*, 89

Objective Content of Human Imagination

"It is a riddle, wrapped in a mystery, inside an enigma; but perhaps there is a key."[141] This comment from Winston Churchill characterizes the task researchers in human imagination face. Much of these explorations have sought to discover and describe the objective content of imagination. Building on Coleridge's model of primary and secondary imagination, Philip Wheelwright offers a model in which the imagination is construed to function cognitively and constructively at once. He suggests four types of imagination with distinct functions: confrontative, stylistic, archetypal, and metaphoric.[142]

Under the rubric of confrontative imagination, Wheelwright emphasizes the evocative power of imaginative language that grabs the attention of the listener by speaking of concrete particulars with directness, immediacy, and precision. His premise is that commonplace language dulls the edges between one experience and another. He asserts, "The first and foremost indispensable attribute of poetic language is its radical particularity of reference, its presentative immediacy. It presents as well as represents; it evokes something of the very quality, tone, and flavor of the concrete with a directness and full experiential relevance."[143]

A key dynamic in preaching is distance from the messenger and the message. Wheelwright coined the term, "stylistic imagination" to point to the poet's ability to create a sense of right distance. Drawing upon stylistic imagination, one strives to give the listener a surprising, sudden view of things from the reverse and unnoticed side. This

---

[141] The Phrase Finder, "The Actions of Russia," Winston Churchill BBC Radio broadcast, October .1939, http://www.phrases.org.uk/meanings/31000.html (accessed January 11, 2009).
[142] Phillip Wheelwright, *The Burning Fountain: A Study in the Language of Symbolism*, 80-100.
[143] Ibid.

element of surprise fosters memorability by creating new and unexpected cognitive connections to the old and familiar.

Golden arches have become a ubiquitous, global image. Like Pavlovian dogs salivating at the sound of the bell, people around the world, even those under the age of three, show immediate recognition of this image and equate it with fast food. Wheelwright might characterize McDonald's golden arches as archetypal imagination. Given the universal recognition of this image, it has come to embody shared meaning across cultures, languages, and geography. Here is an example of archetypal imagination that fuses image and idea where the concrete and general merge. This form of imagination serves as the hinge of shared meaning.

The notion of archetypal imagination offers important implications for preaching. Modern apologists such as Josh McDowell bemoan the erosion of objective truth in postmodern society.[144] Perhaps an alternative and more accurate way to understand postmodern changes in epistemology might focus upon shifts in archetypal images. Biblical images of God's activity in the world that have served for millennia as archetypes for faith are no longer widely known or understood-the cross, light, wind, fire, the empty tomb. In light of the loss of shared images and the sacred meaning they adumbrate, it is unsurprising that folks call into question the language of creeds and dogma.

Images never stand alone. Rather, human imagination combines images in new patterns that build on memory and familiar connections. Wheelwright proposes that metaphoric imagination is at work through the fusion of two or more concrete images, each of which carries emotive and ideational associations. Through this form of

---

[144]Josh McDowell, *Evidence for Christianity* (Nashville: Thomas Nelson, 2006), 18-23.

imagination, humans combine heterogeneous elements with apparently little common ground to form some kind of unity.[145]

The concept of metaphoric imagination lies behind the rabbinical notion of sermons as "stringing pearls." As the Yiddish Song, "Schinerele Perele," suggests, sermons are a collection of pearls of wisdom held together by the thread of common faith.[146] In this vein, sermons are complex extended metaphors. What a contrast this model offers to rhetorical approaches that limit metaphorical imagination to illustrations to bolster the real message of logical points.

David Bryant envisions human imagination as a source of knowledge from three perspectives. For imagination to work, humans must begin with recognition. This is an associative process in which new objects connect with familiar objects in our memory. This connection is vital to naming the world around us. I can name a new article of clothing as a hat because it is like other hats I have seen and worn, even though it differs drastically in color, materials, and design.

Bryant's second imaginative principle is particularity. Humans imagine through perceptive processes. However, we never perceive every aspect of an object, only those attributes available to us from a particular vantage point. Here is the imaginative principle behind the fable of the four blind men and the elephant. Limited only to tactile perception, each blind man comes to a particular imaginative conclusion about the nature of an elephant. Depending on your vantage point, an elephant is rather like a wall, a tree, a snake, or a rope.

---

[145] Phillip Wheelwright, *The Burning Fountain,* 102-104.
[146] Reconstructionist synagogue, Princeton, NJ, "Tradition," http://www.Stringofpearlsweb.org, (accessed March 4, 2009).

Emphasis on the particularity of imagination underlies much of postmodern worldview. Postmodern thinking admits that each one sees the elephant differently and questions whether anyone perceives the whole elephant. To complicate matters further, there is a prior assumption of equanimity. One perception of reality does not trump another for postmodern thinkers. The operative word here is "perception," the subjective, sensory impression of the individual.

In response to this mindset, the poet-gardener approaches preaching from a Pauline perspective, "We live by faith, not sight" (2 Corinthians 5:7). Poet-gardener sermons affirm and seek to reinforce the particular imaginative connection of listeners. And yet, there is no confusion that perception is reality, that each listener should do what is right in his or her own eyes. With the conviction that imagination is the medium, not the source, of revelation, the preacher proclaims a mystery. God alone perceives the whole elephant. Partial and incomplete perceptions of listeners serve as pathways for an encounter with God's completely "other" point of view.

Bryant's third category for imaginative ways of knowing might be characterized as the process of reframing. A logical approach to frames of reference suggests that human development is a process of reframing driven by cognitive activity.[147] People hold certain worldviews or frames influenced by prior experience and knowledge. As new knowledge is acquired, old frames of reference come under interrogation, are found inadequate, and are replaced by new, more accurate ways of understanding the world.

Imaginative reframing draws significantly upon intuitive and heuristic processes. Life experiences confront our worldview. However, the point of contact is not so much

---

[147]David J. Bryant, *Faith and the Play of Imagination: On the Role of Imagination in Religion* (Macon, GA: Mercer University Press, 1989), 36-52.

our thoughts about what the world is like as the metaphors and images we use to make sense of things. A twenty year old woman who has thought of her father as the "rock" in her life is completely disillusioned by the sudden announcement that dad has fallen in love with the office secretary and has left her mother. In her desperation, the young woman prays earnestly for dad to come to his senses, but he continues his errant ways.

Such dislocating experiences require reframing. Dad is clearly not the rock in the way this young woman had imagined him. She wonders about her father: "Who is he? Equally important, who is she in light of these catastrophic events? And, what about the "Rock of Ages" to whom she has prayed? Where is a solid foundation to be found?

Every community of faith includes persons who are going through severe hardship and dislocation of frames of reference. The poet-gardener approaches sermons as strategic opportunities for soul care through imaginative reframing. Sermons are an important way to accompany folks through the reframing process.

Drawing upon the work of Clebsch and Jaekle, the poet-gardener model utilizes imaginative reframing as a modality for the five major movements of pastoral care: healing, sustaining, reconciling, guiding, and transforming.[148] Rather, than presenting logical arguments and "how to" recipes for dealing with existential dilemmas, the preacher offers Biblical images that confront faulty frames of reference and offer redemptive alternatives. In the case of the wayward father and distraught daughter, consider the power of images from Hosea-God faithfully remaining in relationship with God's adulterous spouse.

---

[148]William A. Clebsch and Charles R. Jaekle, *Pastoral Care in Historical Perspective* (Englewood Cliffs, NJ: Prentice-Hall, 1964), 28.

The solidarity and shared meaning the faith community finds in reframing master images for life are relational forms of knowing. By sharing a common imagination for God's presence among us, the congregation accompanies one another in suffering and moves toward healing and Christian maturity. This form of soul care offers grounded support in the midst of suffering. Imaginative reframing builds hope in keeping with the pattern articulated by Paul through which we come to the point that we might "rejoice in our suffering" (Romans 5:3). The poet-gardener offers images of redemptive suffering beyond the excruciating pain of betrayal and unfairness. Rather, folks are empowered to know how to persevere by standing together in a shared vision of "God at work in all things for the good of those who love Him who have been called according to His purpose" (Romans 8:28).

MOVEMENT THREE: SOUL CARE ELEMENTS IN PREACHING

Key Terms for Soul Care Preaching

Poet-gardener preaching is an exercise in soul care. This claim implies a particular way of proclamation with specific goals. More precisely, preaching in a soul care mode involves certain presuppositions about the nature of human beings, the way people grow and develop, and the efficacy of the ministry of preaching in facilitating spiritual growth. These presuppositions are expressed in terms such as soul, soul care, soul care preaching, and spiritual formation. To ensure clarity and precision about poet-gardener preaching, it is important to explore these terms in some detail.

Soul

"We do not have a soul; we are a soul."[149] In reflecting on Biblical categories of soul, Thomas Moore provides a working definition of soul as "The whole person, including the body, but with particular focus on the inner world of thinking, feeling, and willing."[150] This definition points to both the breadth and depth of the term "soul." On the one hand, soul suggests that the spiritual life extends broadly to include all domains of human life. Such a holistic definition challenges the modern tendency toward compartmentalization of human experience into body, mind, and spirit.

On the other hand, "soul" focuses upon the depth dimension of people. To be concerned about the soul is to be willing to go beneath appearances and first impressions, to read between the lines. Categories of the soul presuppose that real, lasting change in

---

David G.Benner, *Care of Souls: Revisioning Christian Nurture and Counsel* (Grand Rapids, MI: Baker Books, 1998), 22.

[149] Thomas Moore, *Care of the Soul: A Guide for Cultivating Depth and Sacredness in Everyday Life* (New York: Harper Collins), 1992, 4.

human life always moves in an "inside-out" pattern, proceeding from the soul, the inner core, and affecting every dimension of a person.[151]

David Benner reclaims Biblical images of humans as creatures with an inextricable depth dimension. In contrast to modern notions of soul as one component part of humans, David Benner suggests that soul is our core identity. In Old Testament usage, the Hebrew term for soul, *nephesh,* does not conceive the soul as a separate spiritual essence or aspect of human life. Rather, *nephesh* draws its meaning from *naphash*, breath of life. To speak of soul in Biblical categories is to point to life itself.

Benner goes on to connect the human soul to creation in the image of God: "Each person is a one of a kind creature made in the image of God. Whatever else the term means, it conveys a sense of enormous dignity and thorough going relationality."[152] To speak of the soul is to claim a core identity for humans as persons in relationship.

Reflecting upon the anthropology embedded in the Genesis stories, Tikva Frymer-Kinsey examines the nuances of Hebrew language for "image of God"-*tselem Elohim.* Although the creation account (Genesis 1:27) does not spell out the meaning of the phrase, "image of God," she proposes several possible connotations of *tselem Elohim* including meanings of dominion granted by God, representation of God, and blessing of God. Referring to Genesis 9:6, "For in the image of God has God made man," Frymer-Kinsey proposes that *tselem* in this context is a statement of the sacred distinctiveness of human life compared to all other creatures.[153]

Soul care

---

[151] Lawrence Crabb, *Inside Out,* 27-29.
[152] David G. Benner, *The Care of Souls: Revisioning Christian Nurture and Counsel*, 36.
[153] Tikya Frymer-Kinsey, *Christianity in Jewish Terms* (New York: Basic Books, 2002), 322-324.

In recent years, preachers, pastoral theologians, and pastoral care specialists have shown renewed interest in the practice of soul care. In part, the revival of soul care comes in reaction against the dominance of quasi-scientific categories for care giving. Jay Adams suggests that the Church has lost her way in the ministry of preaching by adopting the language, presuppositions, and worldview of psychology. With its roots in science and medicine, psychology operates from naturalistic assumptions that abrogate the power of the Gospel. Adams further contends that the Church's fascination with "therapeutic sermons" is little more than "sinners sinfully reflecting on the problem of sin."[154]

Ironically, implications of soul care are embedded in the language of medicine and psychology. Psychiatrist is a transliteration of the Greek, "psuche+iatros," or "healer of the soul." Socrates coined this term to characterize his teaching of students in which he exhorted them to make the care of the soul their chief concern.[155] One should note in Socrates' comment that his focus is on care, not cure. From its ancient origins, soul care focused upon nurture and preservation of well-being. How then, did psychiatry, and even pastoral care, come to be focused upon cure with all of the assumptions of illness and disease that implies?

In many ways, modern healing practices find their starting point more in scientific method than compassion for persons. This statement is not to suggest that those who practice a medical model are devoid of compassion. Nonetheless, personal concern and empathy with people have been relegated to secondary importance. Terms such as "bedside manner" betray this manner of thinking. What matters in a medical model is

---

[154] Jay E. Adams, *Competent to Counsel* (Nashville: P and R Publishing, 1970), 29.
[155] Robert Maynard Hutchings, ed., "Plato's Apology," in Great Books of the Western World, vol. 7, (Chicago: Encyclopedia Britannica, 1952), 206.

precision and measurability, not relationality. From this point of view, skilled practitioners are those who carefully observe the data of human experience, accurately diagnose the problem, and prescribe an effective course of treatment that leads to a cure. The measure of effectiveness in a medical model is incremental relief of symptoms of illness.

By contrast, Thomas Moore speaks of soul care as "the care of persons in their totality, with particular attention to their inner lives."[156] Soul care is fundamentally an act of neighbor love. As Figure 3-1 indicates, soul care includes elements of care (cara) and cure (cura) toward the overarching goal of transformation of the person into the image of Christ.[157]

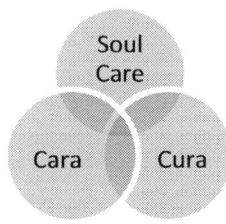

Figure 3-1
Components of Soul Care

Care and cure dynamics may operate simultaneously; the emphasis on one or the other flows out of the needs of the person. Soul care is based on a holistic view of persons. The overlapping circles in Figure 3-1 suggest that human life cannot be neatly divided into component parts. The sum is greater than the whole. Henri Nouwen suggests that discerning how to proceed in soul care requires the wisdom of the Holy Spirit, a deep knowledge of the other, and self-awareness of one's own needs. He observes that the

---

[160] Thomas Moore, *Care of the Soul: A Guide for Cultivating Depth and Sacredness in Everyday Life*, 12.
[161] This diagram draws on the work of David Benner, *Care of Souls,* 21-23.

most difficult part of care of others is diagnosis which literally means "to know through and through" (dia-gnosis).[158]

Gregory the Great conceived of soul care as the shaping of persons through the use of the Scriptures. With reference to preaching, he suggested that the preacher might be compared to a harpist as he or she seeks to care for congregants. "For what are the minds of attentive hearers but the taut strings of a harp which the skillful harpist plays with a variety of strokes that he may not produce a discordant melody because they are not plucked with the same kind of stroke though plucked with the same plectrum."[159] Here Gregory points to two simultaneous movements of soul care in preaching: Building up the community of faith while attending to the needs of individuals. He further suggests the metaphor of gardening for preaching to make his point about multi-tasking in sermons. The preacher must tend the whole garden while keeping a watchful eye on the health and fruitfulness of each plant. In Gregory's language, soul care is a matter of "sowing the Word" by exercise of virtues of insightfulness, self-knowledge, and charity.[160]

Christian soul care finds its origins in ancient practices of Hebrew religion. In the pre-Christian Jewish community, the care of souls occurred within a moral framework that depended upon instruction in the law or Torah. David Benner identifies four classes of care givers within the Hebrew community: priests, scribes, prophets, and wise men. Each class of spiritual leader emphasized certain aspects of soul care. In their leadership of sacrificial rites, priests addressed the need for expiation of guilt. The emergence of a

---

[158] Henri Nouwen, *Creative Ministry*, 49.
[159] Gregory the Great, *Pastoral Care,* Ancient Christian Writers Series, vol. 11, ed. Henry Davis. (Westminster, MD, 1950), 89-90.
[160] Ibid., 86-88.

class of scribes was needed to interpret the body of case law that developed over the centuries. Prophets served a communal role as they called the people as a whole to repentance and reformation of community life. The class of wise men and rabbis cared for souls through preaching-argument and reasoned application of the Scriptures to life. These earliest preachers employed dialogue as their chosen method of soul care, proclaiming principles of the good life through word and deed.[161]

Jesus followed the rabbinical tradition in his preaching ministry; others frequently referred to him as "rabbi" (Mark 9:5, 10:51; John 1:38, 3:2). In keeping with the rabbinical method of teaching, much of Jesus' preaching is dialogical. For example, he tells the parable of the Good Samaritan in the context of a conversation with a scribe who asks, "Who is my neighbor?" (Luke 10: 29-37).

Ironically, Jesus rejects the use of the term "rabbi." At first blush, the rationale for this prohibition seems to be a correction of excesses of pride among religious leaders (Matthew 23:7). However, there is also a second motivation for Jesus' command to avoid this title. He points to the deformation of relationships involved in honorific titles and the pecking order among people that the use of such titles implies. Instead, Jesus emphasizes a redemptive pattern of relationships among his followers: "One Master . . . all brothers . . . one Teacher, the Christ" (Matthew 23: 8-10). To preach is not to dominate people, but rather to dialogue with them in an egalitarian exchange that is mutually edifying.

This exploration of soul care in the context of preaching would be incomplete without some comments about reconciliation. As noted earlier, postmodern philosophers and sociologists speak in one voice about the sense of alienation and yearning for

---

[161] David G. Benner, *The Care of Souls: Revisioning Christian Nurture and Counsel*, 26.

community among postmodern people. Before the preacher can offer her or his listeners guidance in faith, the gap of mistrust must be bridged. In order for the preacher to care for souls, he or she must welcome people, create a safe space for the exploration of faith, and listen to their viewpoints.

Welcoming people into the company of God and the faith community is important, but it is only the beginning. Reconciliation requires initiative in the face of resistance, patience to wait on the timid, and tough love to confront stiff-necked persons. Clebsch and Jaekle suggest that reconciliation involves two primary movements: forgiveness and discipline.[162]

Across two millennia, the Church has devoted significant effort to understanding how reconciliation works. Commenting on the subject, Tertullian suggested four main elements of reconciliation: preparation, confession, penance, and restoration.[163] His incisive analysis of reconciliation suggests that it is a complex community process requiring time and perseverance. The challenge to the preacher is to discern how the proclamation of the Word supports reconciliation as a core element of soul care.

Soul care preaching

Building upon the thoughts of Augustine, Gregory labeled preaching as an exercise in guidance of souls or "psychagogy." For him, all preaching is soul care preaching. Gregory characterizes sermons as more pastoral discourse than rhetoric, more like a parent's guidance to children than a commander's orders to the troops. Psychagogy at its essence is a form of spiritual direction empowered by deep love and including elements of forgiveness, moral instruction, and exhortation. As he attempts to describe

---

[162] William Clebsch and Charles Jaekle, *Pastoral Care in Historical Perspective*, 56-66.
[163] Ibid., 59.

how God is at work in caring for souls through preaching, Gregory suggests that the Son is the Word of God and the Holy Spirit is the tongue to speak the Word. Through the Word, God seeks to enkindle passionate love for divine wisdom and to evoke moral transformation, a renewed capacity to desire what God desires within the community of Christ.[164]

In Gregory's model, soul care preaching entails two responses to God: contemplation and moral action.[165] In other words, the virtuous life springs from the heart bathed in the Word of God. He further emphasizes that the preacher cannot stand as an observer outside of God's activity while impassively directing others to turn to God. Instead, the preacher must be a person whose life is immersed in the Scripture. His or her external authority in the pulpit is driven by internal virtue. Here, Gregory is deeply informed by Augustine's notion that preachers must become "living sermons."[166]

Gregory suggests that a preacher is one who has been formed by scripture into a certain kind of person who possesses the judgment to speak the Word to people in all conditions. Preaching involves a "knowing how" in which the preacher speaks language "of" faith, not "about" faith. Those who proclaim the Word must possess a lived wisdom in which doctrine and life are one.[167]

Reflecting on Jesus' earliest sermon recorded in Matthew, Gregory insists that the main aim of preaching is calling people to return to God. "Repent, for the Kingdom of heaven is near." (Matthew 4:17). In lived reality, returning to God entails processes of putting off vices and putting on virtues toward the goal of perfection in Christ. Toward

---

[164] Michael Pasquarello, III, *Sacred Rhetoric: Classic Images in Preaching* (Grand Rapids: Zondervan, 2005), 42.
[165] Ibid., 39.
[166] Augustine of Hippo. "De Doctrina Christiana," cited in *Sacred Rhetoric,* 41.
[167] Michael Pasquarello, III, *Sacred Rhetoric,* 39-46.

this end, he insists that the preacher must know not only the language but also the grammar of faith. That is to say, God's Word provides both the details of action and the overarching order for the godly life.[168]

Reflecting on necessary qualities for effective preachers, Gregory suggests that humble obedience is the primary virtue. On the one hand, preachers must know how Christian speech works to create and sustain the life of faith. On the other hand, one who preaches must remain on guard against arrogance or pride of speech. The faithful preacher remembers at all times that God alone can change human hearts.[169]

In giving his personal testimony, The Reverend Michael Moore commented: "I committed my life to Christ in response to a sermon given by Pastor Charles Lever on an ordinary Sunday morning in July. I had never met Pastor Lever. I'm sure he had no idea that God was speaking to me, to me personally and profoundly, through his sermon. But God did. And my life has never been the same."[170] This testimony underlines the relational dynamics of soul care as a personal, intimate experience with God.

David Benner suggests that the efficacy of soul care grows out of "deep knowing," a true intimacy with Christ. However, this should not be misconstrued as promoting a "me and my Jesus" approach to Christian spirituality. Deep knowledge of God and self occur in the context of a hospitable, supportive faith community. Quoting an Ubuntu proverb, Benner suggests that one cannot receive soul care and the personal healing that accompanies it outside of a community context: "I am because we are; we

---

[168] Michael Pasquarello, III, *Sacred Rhetoric*, 39-46.
[169] Ibid.
[170] Michael Moore, "Public Testimony to the Florida Annual Conference of the United Methodist Church," (sermon, Daytona Beach, FL, June 11, 2009).

are because I am."[171] Soul care entails discovery of the unique self that God ordained one to be. But it also involves integration into a loving community where persons find not only support but also opportunity to serve others.

Michael Moore's testimony also underlines the fact that soul care operates by God's initiative. Soul care comes as a response of the human spirit to initiative of the Holy Spirit. Benner points to the universal need for hope-hope that life might be different, hope for a second chance-as the energizing dynamic that creates readiness to respond to God. The great paradox in soul care is that people cannot accomplish the desired change through their own efforts. Surrender is the critical moment of transformation.[172]

Spiritual Formation

If soul care is the essential work of poet-gardener preaching, spiritual formation is the goal. To speak of spiritual formation in preaching is to suggest that the poet-gardener proclaims the Word with an outcome in mind. That desired outcome of sermons is character formation, or more precisely, transformation of persons into the image of Christ. Paul uses the language of holiness and the metaphor of washing to point to ways Christ is transforming the Church through his Word: "Christ loved the Church and gave himself up for her to make her holy, cleansing her by the washing with water through the word" (Ephesians 5:26).

The Carmelite community has traditionally practiced the "Tripudium" processional form for worship as a way of symbolizing the nature of Christian spiritual formation. In this processional form, community members make their way into the

---

[171] David G. Benner, *Care of Souls*, 101.
[172] Ibid, 126.

sanctuary by taking two steps forward and one step back.[173] In humility, this faith community is acknowledging that spiritual formation is an imperfect journey toward perfection in Christ. One becomes Christ-like through processes of forgiveness, suffering, and grace. Taken all together, spiritual formation resembles more a spiraling, rhythmic pattern of movement toward God than an instantaneous makeover. As the preacher proclaims the Word week to week, he or she aims to keep the congregation in step with the Spirit and moving toward God.

Dating from the sixth century writings of Pseudo-Dionysius (c. 550), Church fathers spoke of spiritual formation as a three-fold pattern of purgation, illumination, and union. Dionysius suggests that the "three ways" are universal to human experience. His model is one of divine-human cooperation in which spiritual growth is both thearchic (divine origin) and anthroarchic (human effort). And, he casts the "three ways" as a fixed pattern of successive steps toward progression in Christ.[174]

Benedict, and Bernard of Clairvaux built their understanding of spiritual formation on the notion of the three ways. Bernard refines the model by suggesting that the spiritual life is like climbing a ladder to God. His metaphor includes twelve steps of humility and pride that may lead upward to union with Christ or downward into fleshly living. Here Bernard articulates the truth that even the most casual observer of human nature sees: character formation is far from linear, steady progress.[175]

---

[173] St. Gregory Episcopal Church. "Sarx," http://raphael.doxos.com/2008/06/28/tripudium-proccession-to-the-table-and-transfer-of-gifts, (accessed August 20, 2009).

[174] Earnest E. Larkin, "The Three Spiritual Ways." http://www.carmelnet.org, 2008, (accessed March 16, 2009).

[175] Gillian R. Evans, "On the Steps of Humility and Pride," *Bernard of Clairvaux: Selected Works*, The Classics of Western Spirituality (Mahwah, N.J.: Paulist Press, 1987), 99-144.

The poet-gardener preaches weekly with the knowledge that the maturity of the faith community is a work in progress. Some weeks, people have taken the next step up the ladder toward perfection in Christ. It is a time of great celebration and thankfulness for God's grace. At other times, repentance within the context of forgiveness is the order of the day. Henri Nouwen conceptualized this rhythm of spiritual formation in preaching as a pattern of oscillation among three poles of spiritual development. Drawing upon the Great Command (Luke 10:27), Nouwen suggests that spiritual formation consists of a pattern of three movements as depicted in Figure 3-2.

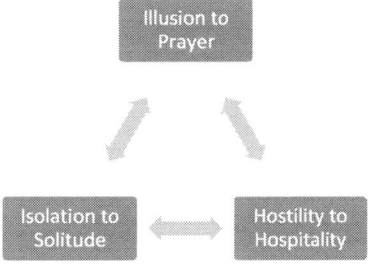

Figure 3-2
Three Movements of the Spiritual Life

Nouwen's major contribution to an understanding of spiritual formation lies in his notion of the holistic nature of human growth. As Figure 3-2 suggests, spiritual formation is an integrated experience in which growth or shrinkage in one dimension of the spiritual life impacts all others. One cannot become Christ-like by compartmentalized spiritual practices.[176]

Eugene Peterson summarizes the challenges of spiritual formation through preaching.

"You would think that believing that Jesus is God among us would be the hardest thing. It is not. It turns out that the hardest thing is to believe that God's work is all

---

[176] Henri Nouwen, *Reaching Out: The Three Movements of the Spiritual Life* (New York: Doubleday, 1975), 12-17.

happening in and under the conditions of our humanity. The perpetual threat to living a real life, an authentic and true and honest life, is to evade or dump this man, this Jesus, this ordinary way he comes to us and this inglorious company he keeps. (We are tempted) to pretentiously attempt to be our own god or to fashion a glamorous god or gods that appeal to our vanity."[177]

Preaching promotes spiritual formation by introducing and re-introducing persons to Christ. Such a model moves the preacher away from "how to" sermons in favor of "Have I told you lately about Jesus?" The poet-gardener preaches with the conviction that transformational sermons are fundamentally relational. By promoting a deeper and more authentic relationship with Jesus, the preacher partners with God in the formation of a Christ-like community.

---

[177] Eugene H. Peterson, *Christ Plays in Ten Thousand Places: A Conversation in Spiritual Theology* (Grand Rapids, MI: Eerdmans, 2005), 34-36.

The Rhythm of Soul Care

Since we live by the Spirit, let us keep in step with the Spirit (Galatians 5:25).

In his sermon, *A Plain Account of Christian Perfection,* John Wesley exhorted his followers to continually ask of one another, "Are you moving on to perfection?"[178] He utilized this notion of lifelong journey as a way to conceptualize spiritual formation. In a similar way, the poet-gardener model builds on the premise that spiritual formation is more a rhythmic process than a linear progression. Figure 3-3 illustrates the rhythm of soul care.

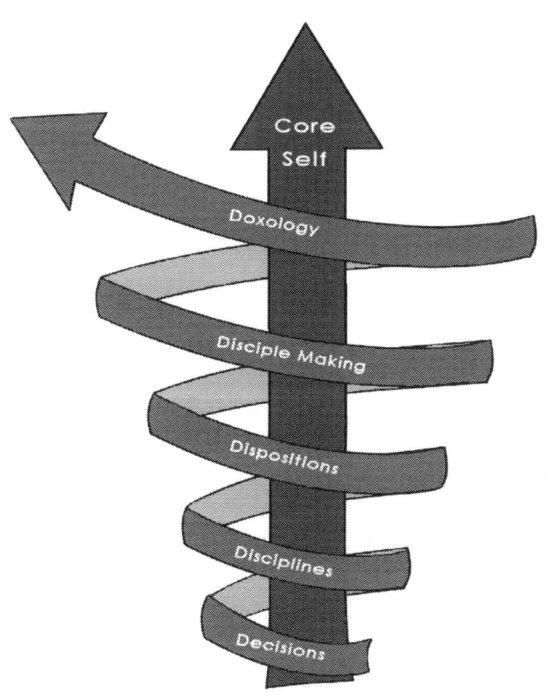

Figure 3-3: The Rhythm of Soul Care

Discipleship in Christ involves the maturation of the core self of a person through the development of deeper and more authentic relationships with God, self, and neighbor.

---

[178] Thomas Jackson, ed., *The Works of John Wesley,* vol.. 11, no. 29 (Grand Rapids, MI: Baker), 2000, 366-446.

In psychological language, theorists speak of human development as entailing twin processes of individuation and integration. Individuation processes are represented in Diagram 3-3 by the red arrow labeled, "core self." The blue spiral depicts human growth through integration in the Body of Christ. Individuation and integration operate mutually. One cannot become a healthy individual in isolation. As the African proverb goes, "It takes a village to raise a child."

Robert Kegan suggests that human development might be represented by a spiral-shaped pattern representing growth through a process of adaptation to increasingly complex challenges in life.[179] In a similar way, Figure 3-3 pictures spiritual growth as a winding spiral path toward the goal of formation in the image of Christ. The spiral provides a three-dimensional view of Christian discipleship. The spiral moves steadily upward toward God. At the same time, it is an imperfect, circuitous way that includes setbacks as well as forward movement.

In a sense, humans traverse the same ground of life again and again, confronting the same challenges repeatedly over the course of a lifetime. And yet, the growing person does not encounter circumstances in the same way over time. The third dimension of the spiral-the expanding, outward moving coil-suggests that our maturing lives move out to join the community in shared strength.

In my first assignment in parish ministry, I was shocked by my encounter with an elderly man who had been a church leader for almost fifty years. Despite his long-term involvement in the church and active leadership in a variety of important roles, this man was full of anger and bitterness. As a brand new pastor, I discovered the surprising truth

---

[179] Robert Kegan, *The Evolving Self: Problem and Process in Human Development* (Cambridge, MA: Harvard University Press), 1986, 11-24.

that spiritual maturity requires more than simply the passage of time in the church. To be chronologically aged is not the same as being mature. Growth in Christ requires a process of intentionality.

The poet-gardener model builds upon an intentional process of formation involving the five movements labeled in Figure 3-3: Decisions, disciplines, dispositions, disciple-making, and doxology. To map the spiritual transformation process in this way is to suggest that human cooperation with God's grace takes different forms depending on the life challenges and maturity level of persons. Each of these movements entails aspects of the others.

It should also be noted that no claims are made that this map fully captures the complexity of lived human experience. Often, human beings are engaged in multiple processes simultaneously, making decisions that reflect dispositions and require discipline. Further, the model might be misconstrued to suggest a fixed sequential order for spiritual formation vis a vis Erickson's model for human development or Kohlberg's stages of moral development. The poet-gardener model does not suggest that all people move through a fixed, predictable pattern of spiritual maturation. As Jesus pointed out, "The wind blows wherever it pleases. You hear its sound, but you cannot tell where it comes from or where it is going. So it is with everyone born of the Spirit" (John 3:8).

*The Anatomy of **Decisions** in Preaching*

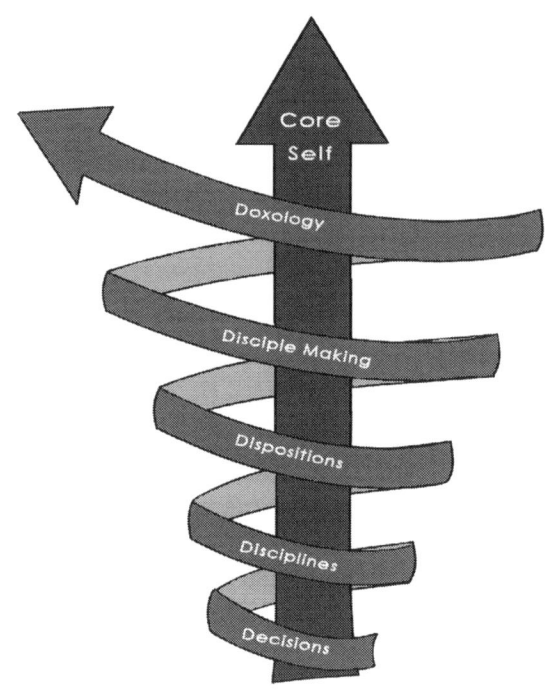

Figure 3-3: The Rhythm of Soul Care

If one asks an evangelical pastor how things are going in her or his church, the likely response will involve an accounting of the number of decisions for Christ over the past year. Of course, leading persons to decisions of commitment to God is a key part of pastoral work. But what is the anatomy of decisions, particularly transformative decisions that involve a change in core values and commitments?

"No one can come to me unless the Father who sent me draws him" (John 6:44). In these words of Jesus, he affirms that our spiritual decisions actually begin in the mind of God. Reflecting on this principle, John Wesley built on the thinking of Augustine and Arminius to articulate the concept of prevenient grace, God going before us and enabling our human ability to accept grace. In his sermon, "On Working Out Our Own Salvation," John Wesley describes prevenient grace as "The first wish to please God, the first dawn of light concerning His will, and the first slight transient conviction of having sinned against Him."[180] In other words, the Scriptural witness affirms that spiritual decisions are always more than human agency or pure exercises of free will. Decisions of commitment to Christ are a cooperation of the human will with the divine will.

What role, then, does preaching play in facilitating spiritual decisions? The temptation is to focus on the art of persuasion, devoting the bulk of one's effort to making compelling, convincing arguments for right belief. Jesus' formula for decision making is much more personal and straight forward: "When I am lifted up from the earth, (I) will draw all men to myself" (John 12:32). In recording these words of Jesus, John is quick to add the commentary, "He said this to show the kind of death he was going to die" (John 12:33).

Soul care sermons operate out of the magnetic power of the crucified LORD. Beyond any human arguments for decisions of commitment to God, the cross is the convincing evidence of God's prior love for all humanity. Here is the drawing power of Jesus that empowers preaching.

If soul care preaching is a vehicle for God's prevenient grace, it is also an expression of the liberating power of faith in Christ. In fact, Paul points to freedom in Christ as the only true liberation from spiritual bondage. "It is for freedom that Christ has set us free. Stand firm, then, and do not let yourselves be burdened again by a yoke of slavery" (Galatians 5:1).

At the most fundamental level, decisions are an expression of freedom. In common parlance, decisions are defined as acts of independence and private choices. The

---

[180] John Wesley and Kenneth Collins, "On Working Out Our Own Salvation," *Wesley on Salvation: A Study in the Standard Sermons* (Grand Rapids: Zondervan, 1989), 85-91.

Biblical context suggests that faith decisions are an act of covenant in which we cooperate with God's grace. In fact, spiritual decisions represent a transformation of the mind (Romans 12:2) in which God is setting aside the slavery to the sinful mind in favor of thinking with the mind led by the Holy Spirit. On this subject, Gerald May characterizes spiritual decisions as "an active attempt to live life in accord with the facts of grace."[181]

Figure 3-4 depicts human decisions as covenantal acts involving six key elements: Grace, honesty, repentance, dignity, responsibility, and community.

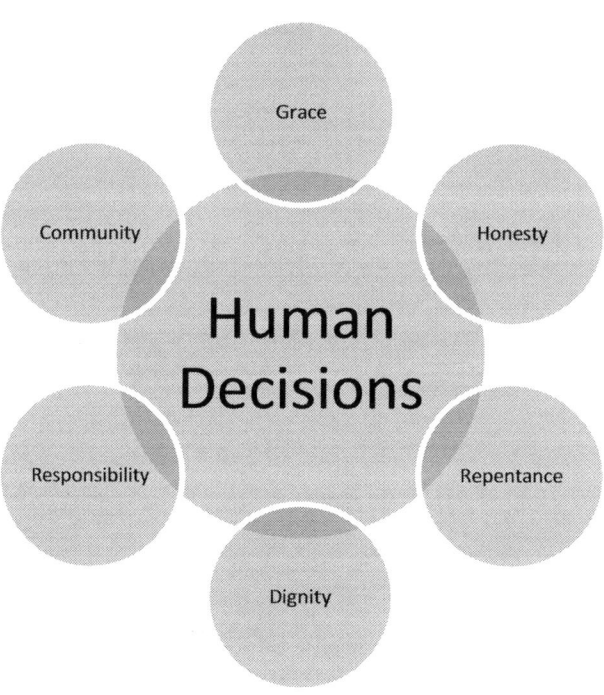

Figure 3-4 The Anatomy of Decisions

If poet-gardener sermons are to affect spiritual decisions, they must be experiences of grace. Before persons are ready to risk change or commitment or lifestyle, they must experience God's unqualified love for them. Henri Nouwen suggests that the

---

[181] Gerald G. May, *Addiction and Grace: Love and Spirituality in the Healing of Addictions*, 127.

story of the baptism of Jesus provides a vivid example of the human need for grace as a precedent to living out a life devoted to God. At his baptism, Jesus heard the voice of God speaking, "You are my beloved Son in whom I am well pleased" (Matthew 3:17). God's affirmation of Jesus as "The Beloved" came as a free expression of God's heart toward him before he had begun his public ministry or done anything to warrant affirmation. In the same way, Nouwen suggests that hearing God's affirmation, "You are my beloved," becomes an open door to a profoundly different direction in life:

> "Every time you listen with great attentiveness to the voice that calls you the beloved, you will discover within yourself a desire to hear that voice longer and more deeply. It is like discovering a well in the desert. Once you have touched wet ground, you want to dig deeper."[182]

According to the gospel of Matthew, Jesus' first sermon was a call to spiritual decisions: "Repent, for the kingdom of heaven is near" (Matthew 4:17). "Metanoia," the Greek word translated as repentance, suggests changing one's heart or mind about someone or something.[183] And yet, the poet-gardener recognizes that repentance is far more than a rational, intellectual process. Repentance involves the conscience, that element of human functioning that engages in moral discernment. Spiritual decisions involve not only a rational analysis of the truthfulness and weight of alternatives, but also more intuitive insights about the rightness or wrongness of situations.

Dating from the thought of Augustine, the Christian church has conceived of conscience along two important dimensions. Augustine described the conscience as "a truly primitive faculty . . . it is a particular manner of feeling which corresponds to the goodness of moral actions, as taste is a manner of feeling which corresponds to beauty."

---

[182] Henri Nouwen, Henri, *Life of the Beloved*, 31.
[183] W. E. Vine, *Vine's Expository Dictionary of Old and New Testament Words* (Nashville: Thomas Nelson, 2003), 1081.

In contrast to this notion of conscience as primitive and largely intuitive, the Church has also held conscience to be the highest human function, "the palace of Christ, the temple of the Holy Ghost."[184] As the Holy Spirit works in the conscience, persons experience conviction, sorrow for sin, and resolve to do the right thing.

The conscience facilitates authentic decisions as it demands honesty with God and self. Such honesty requires self-awareness, including awareness of the tendency toward self-deception. In a sense, it is the experience of grace that gives one the courage to be honest about sin. With a dawning awareness of God's gracious character, persons are empowered to take a risk, the risk of accepting their fallenness and need for change. As Gerald May put it, "Honesty risks that God is good."[185] Self-awareness is the beginning of a greater transparency in which persons move beyond the fearful impulse to hide their sins from God and self and bring them into the light.

Soul care preaching promotes moments of honest insight that might grow into long-term patterns of consistency, constancy, and steadiness. Of course, a spiritual epiphany holds little value for transformation if it does not lead to a cycle of change. Decisions without the disciplines to make them a lived reality are little more than good intentions. Here the spiraling rhythm of soul care comes to bear. Honesty replaces self-deception as a disposition or character attribute only as one habitually practices honest decisions through disciplines of self-examination, confession, and accountability.

If honesty involves taking the risk that God is good, dignity risks that humans have a core of goodness that cannot be obliterated.[186] Dignity is that element of decisions

---

[184] Augustine of Hippo, *The Confessions of St. Augustine* (Grand Rapids: Revell, 2008), 208.
[189] Gerald G. May, *Addiction and Grace, 169.*

[186] Gerald G. May, *Addiction and Grace, 169.*

that expresses faith in oneself. Gregory the Great pointed to elements of dignity in decisions in his reference to the timid, those frozen in fear and self-images of shame and worthlessness.[187]

On a broader scale, all persons suffer with some level of shame. Psychologists note that people express shame in paradoxical ways, some in self-deprecation others in arrogance. Shame cuts to the core of persons, calling into question one's basic worth as a person. John Ortberg suggests that shame is particularly toxic in that it operates out of the faulty thinking, "There is something fundamentally wrong with me."[188] The antidote to shame in its various forms is found in claiming one's God-given dignity as God's beloved.

Taking responsibility is a critical component of decisions that involves internal and external actions. The primary internal action is accurate attribution of responsibility. In taking responsibility, one stops blaming others and affirms, "I have sinned." Karl Menninger suggests that true healing of thoughts and emotions requires accurate attribution of responsibility as the first step.[189] More precisely, one cannot fully practice forgiveness without perceiving one's own part in sinful behavior and attitudes. Jesus' parable of the Pharisee and the publican (Luke 18:9-14) points to this principle. Jesus tells this parable as a correction to "some who were confident of their own righteousness and looked down on everybody else" (Luke 18:9). These misguided people attributed no wrongdoing to themselves while assuming the worst about others. The spiritual decision to follow Christ involves taking responsibility for one's own sinfulness while avoiding

---

[191] Gregory the Great, *Pastoral Care,* 3.36
[192] John Ortberg, *The Life You've Always Wanted,* 168.
[193] Karl Menninger, *Whatever Became of Sin?* (New York: Bantam Books, 1978), 21-23.

attributing blame to others. As Bonhoeffer put it, "We have learned a bit too late in the day that action springs not from thought but from a readiness for responsibility."[190]

Billy was a friend of mine during my college years who made a commitment to Christ during a local summer revival. The next day he announced to me, "I got saved last night." I was pleased for Billy, but also curious to see what difference "being saved" might make in his life. In my observation, there was no discernible difference. Billy continued with the same worldly attitudes, the same manner of speech and behavior, the same life goals as before his spiritual decision. Finally, my curiosity got the best of me. "Billy, what's different in your life since you got saved?" I asked. "I've been saved from my sins and guaranteed a place in heaven," he responded. Unsatisfied with this answer, I queried further: "What about now?" Billy's answer betrayed a missing element in his spiritual formation. "Now? Like I said, I'm free from my sins. I can live my life as I please with no more guilt."

Billy and the pastor under whose teaching he had come to faith were missing the basic element of lived responsibility in spiritual decisions. Spiritual decisions remain at the level of good intentions unless and until they become reality through responsible, external action. Many Christian sermons exhort the people to come to the altar and give their lives to Christ. However, this is the alpha of spiritual formation, not the omega.

Billy and all Christians require a community in order to make and keep spiritual decisions. Through the community of faith, the Word is preached and Christ invites us "Come unto me" (Matthew 11:28). Equally, the faith community is the context in which one receives soul care. Spiritual decisions require the support of others in the form of guidance, encouragement, and accountability.

---

[190] Dietrich Bonhoeffer, *Letters and Papers from Prison* (New York: Touchstone, 1997), 137.

In western society where radical individualism is the prevailing worldview, community dimensions of spiritual decisions often elude us. As soul care preaching calls people to a decision to follow Christ, the poet-gardener also emphasizes that we are incapable of faithful discipleship alone. Dietrich Bonhoeffer suggests that we hear not only a word of salvation but an equally compelling call of responsibility when the Word is preached : "From God we hear the word: 'If you want my goodness to stay with you then serve your neighbor, for that is where God comes to you.' "[191]

---

[191] Dietrich Bonhoeffer, *No Rusty Swords: Letters, Lectures, and Notes 1928-1936 from the Collected Works of Dietrich Bonhoeffer,* vol. 1, ed. and trans. Edwin H. Robertson and John Bowden.(New York: Harper and Row, 1965), 32.

*The Anatomy of **Disciplines** in Preaching*

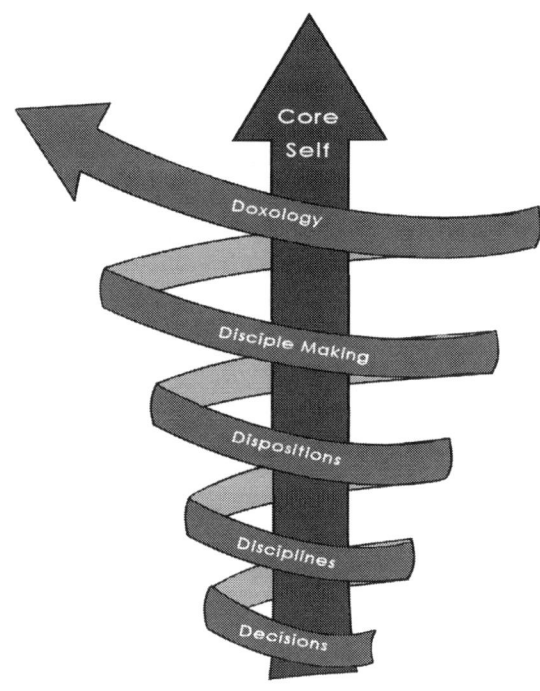

Figure 3-3 The Rhythm of Soul Care

"A disciplined person is one who can do the right thing in the right way at the right time for the right reason and in the right spirit."[192] In this practical definition, John Ortberg suggests that spiritual disciplines entail a holistic regimen of training. Soul care preaching addresses all aspects of human functioning, not simply the spiritual.

If spiritual disciplines are training for the life we have always wanted, why do preachers encounter significant resistance to elements of discipline? For many, discipline and punishment are synonymous. Discipline is viewed in a negative light as unpleasant activity or suffering intended to make one a better person. Even the writer of Hebrews reinforces this point of view. "No discipline seems pleasant at the time, but painful. Later

---

[192] John Ortberg, *The Life You've Always Wanted*, 46.

on, however, it produces a harvest of righteousness and peace for those who have been trained by it" (Hebrews 12:11).

Disciplines do involve methodical training that disturbs one's comfort and habits, inflicting some measure of pain. But there is another dimension to disciplines. In a profound sense, spiritual disciplines are training for freedom, the freedom to follow God as God may lead without constraint of fearfulness, ignorance, or guilt. The poet-gardener offers spiritual disciplines to the congregation as a way of freedom to keep in step with the Spirit.

Discipline of Doing the Right Thing

"Hope begins in the dark, the stubborn hope that if you just show up and do the right thing, the dawn will come. You wait, and watch, and work. You don't give up."[193]

What qualifies an action as the "right thing?" Certainly, right things comport with God's will. When Christians pray the disciples' prayer, "Thy will be done," doing the right thing is the focus. If this prayer is to be a spiritual discipline beyond recitation of a memorized formula, then it must become more action prayer than rhetoric.[194] As the community prays, "Thy will be done," Christians seek God's empowerment to act under the guidance of divine will in all areas of life.

Doing the right thing requires that one practice a certain kind of prayer. Dallas Willard conceives of the discipline of prayer in terms of a conversational relationship with God. He suggests that one prays most effectively in a rhythm of dialogue with God that mirrors patterns of discourse with a cherished friend. In Willard's estimation, meaningful conversation doesn't just happen; it requires work and practice. Through the

---

[193] Anne Lamott, *Bird by Bird: Some Instructions on Writing and Life* (New York: Anchor, 1995), 9.

[194] Terry Tekyl, *Making Room to Pray* (Anderson, IN: Bristol, 1999), 25.

course of conversational prayer, disciples discover the mind and heart of God at a new level.[195] Doing the right thing is a natural extension of the life spent in on-going communication with God.

Jesus spoke of doing the right thing in terms of obedience that produces fruit, "fruit that will last" (John 15:16). The fruitful life requires the discipline of obedience and a focus on the ends. Keeping the end in mind is both a matter of discerning what is best and resisting the draw of temporary, quick fixes. This is a particularly challenging set of dynamics in postmodern society that prizes the immediate solution.

Michael Brown points to the principle of "acherit" as an ancient Hebrew discipline for doing the right thing. "Acherit" is an English transliteration for the Hebrew phrase, "in the end." The writer of Proverbs admonishes the young man: "There is a way that seems right to a man, but in the end, it leads to death" (Proverbs 14:12, 16:25). These proverbs commend the discipline of reflection before action.[196] What seems to be the right thing often is not. The key question is: How will this turn out in the end?

Perhaps the greatest challenge in Christian discipleship is perseverance. Paul speaks of perseverance as the great "if" of the fruitful life. "Let us not become weary in doing good for at the proper time we will reap a harvest *if* we do not give up" (Galatians 6:9, emphasis by the author). Doing the right thing is more a consistent pattern of right living than isolated episodes of correct behavior.

Ironically, perseverance is learned through the spiritual discipline of smallness. Rather than focusing on spiritual heroics, smallness trains one to serve God and others in

---

[195] Dallas Willard, *Hearing God: Developing a Conversational Relationship with God* (Downers Grove, IL: InterVarsity, 1999), 37-40.
[196] Michael L. Brown, "In the End." (Sermon, Brownsville Assembly of God Church, Pensacola, Florida, October, 1999).

anonymity, behind the scenes. In smallness, one comes to value the importance of incremental progress as Kingdom victories. Through this discipline, disciples learn to say "no" to the temptation to grandiosity on the one hand or despair on the other.[197]

Discipline of Doing Things the Right Way

In establishing worship as the central act of covenant with God's people, God provided Moses with a highly detailed prescription for the tabernacle and its furnishings (Exodus 25-30). The command to build the tabernacle included a call to do it the right way: "Make this tabernacle and all its furnishings exactly like the pattern I will show you" (Exodus 25: 9). In the case of the Hebrew people, God used the vision given to Moses on Mount Sinai to guide them in the right way. Centuries later, Solomon prayed for divine wisdom for the people, "Teach them the right way to live" (2 Chronicles 6:27). In lived reality, God's people were called to fear of the LORD as motivation for living the right way with diligence and attention to detail.

In both the Old and New Testaments, the Bible commends the discipline of fear of the LORD as the path to righteousness, living the right way. The Hebrew term for righteousness, *tseh'-dek,* is a juridical term that envisions God as the judge of life and includes elements of straightness, integrity, and justice. The righteous life is the straight life in accord with the divine plan.[198]

New Testament theology expands the concept of righteousness (*dikaiosune*) to the person of Jesus. He is the fulfillment and embodiment of righteousness.[199] The right way

---

[197] John Ortberg, *The Life You've Always Wanted*, 171-184.
[198] James Strong, *Strong's Exhaustive Concordance of the Bible* (Nashville: Thomas Nelson, 1996), 6664.
[199] Ibid.

in life becomes a matter of carefully following Jesus: "I am the way, and the truth, and the life" (John 14:6).

Many people operate under the faulty notion that the nature of righteousness shifted with the coming of Jesus, leaving behind God's judgment and replacing it with grace. Ronald Allen points out that this bifurcation of the Scriptures into a legalistic old covenant and a graceful new covenant leads to the rejection of the Old Testament as an outdated, non-applicable message. And, it contributes to a false sense that one can live well without fear of the LORD. [200]

Eugene Peterson suggests that fear of the LORD might best be understood as, "A way of life in which human feelings and behavior are fused with God's being and revelation." This definition refines fear of the LORD in more familial categories as it points to the dynamic of right living that flows out an accurate understanding of God as Father and one's relationship to God as child. In this sense, fear of the LORD is driven by love of God without any misguided notions of equanimity with God.[201]

Postmodern worldview favors egalitarian relationships in every domain. In a sense, postmodern suspicion of authority extends even to God. And yet, it is a dangerous heresy to portray humans as autonomous creatures who are accountable to no one except the self. This widespread misapprehension promotes significant resistance to the concept of fear of the LORD. Acknowledging these levels of resistance, the poet-gardener avoids scare tactics in an attempt to engender the fear of God in the people. Rather, he or she models the discipline of fear of the LORD. Sermons are delivered in meekness, not out of

---

[200] Ronald J. Allen and John C. Holbert, *Holy Root, Holy Branches: Christian Preaching from the Old Testament* (Nashville: Abingdon Press, 1995), 109-111.

205 Eugene H. Peterson, *Christ Plays in Ten Thousand Places: A Conversation in Spiritual Theology*, 41-43.

anxiety about the reactions of the people, but with an awareness of the sacredness of the task of preaching. Even more, the personhood of the preacher must be that of a God-fearing person. Qualities of knowledge, wisdom, and understanding in sermons must flow out of the consistent lived pattern of fear of the LORD. "The fear of the LORD is the beginning of knowledge" (Proverbs 1:7).

In a recent conversation, a ministerial colleague compared preaching to a stand-up comedian act. My immediate reaction to this image was a combination of revulsion and generalized anxiety. Certainly, humor and playfulness have a role in preaching, even a strategic role, in engaging the congregation. And yet, the image of the stand-up comedian is woefully inadequate for preaching. The point of preaching is never to get people to laugh. Preaching deals with the person of Jesus Christ and all of the sacredness that comes with his presence. How might soul care preaching be joyful while appropriately expressing fear of the LORD? The image of the wise fool points to the ironic role of the preacher as God fearing person who also takes the risk of proclaiming the Word in playful ways. This image is explored in depth in Movement Four of the book.

In many ways, fear of the LORD is as much the way one preaches as what one preaches. Through intentional use of tone and mood, the poet-gardener signals the gravity of the message and the seriousness with which listeners should receive it. A number of sermonic elements work together to express a tone of reverence: voice inflection, slower pace, facial expression, and careful choice of words.[202] Here the preacher models a way for the faith community to treat God's Word as distinct from human words, deserving special consideration and thoughtful response. The discipline of fear of the LORD develops the ability to hear the gospel as good news from a loving God who is also holy and righteous.

---

[202] Fred B. Craddock, *Preaching*, 145-147.

Discipline of Doing Things at the Right Time

"Therefore Jesus told them, 'The right time for me has not yet come; for you any time is right'" (John 7:6). Jesus comments about the right time to act in response to his brothers' mocking about going up to Jerusalem where he might display his glory. And, this comment comes in the context of unbelief, "Even his own brothers did not believe in him" (John 7:5). The practice of faith requires the discipline of right timing, or more precisely, discerning God's timing to act.

When I applied for ordination in the United Methodist Church in 1986, the Board of Ordained Ministry responded "not at this time" to my application. To my utter dismay and disappointment, the ordination board postponed my ordination for a year. They asked that I spend the year reflecting on a single question: "How do you experience grace?" In retrospect, this action by the Board of Ordained Ministry showed great spiritual wisdom. They were sensitive to the discipline of right timing. These leaders understood that one's actions become fruitful for God only by keeping in step with the Spirit and acting in accord with God's timing.

Quite often, right timing requires a season of waiting on the LORD. The Bible is full of admonitions to wait on the LORD. "Be still before the LORD and wait patiently for him" (Psalm 37:7). Waiting is a much neglected discipline in the twenty-first century; speed is a highly prized commodity. In all forms of transportation, communication, even decision making, time is measured more in seconds than in minutes or hours. In common parlance, waiting is considered to be lost productivity, a waste of time.

David Yonggi Cho conceives of preaching as a time of waiting on the LORD. According to Cho, Korean churches follow a standard pattern of worship in which a period of quiet meditation and waiting on the LORD follows the sermon. In this practice, the church is actively listening for a word from God. The community of faith acknowledges that hearing from God cannot be rushed or forced.

By contrast, Cho writes of his experience in traveling to America as the preacher for a revival meeting. He recounts his experience of traveling six thousand miles to speak at a worship gathering that had been three years in the planning.

"I traveled around the world at great expense to my hosts and my home congregation only to be told that I should limit my sermon to twenty minutes. The revival began with much spirited singing and several solos. I preached, and then, without the slightest pause, the worship leader introduced another soloist. The people were given hardly enough time to breathe, let alone meditate on the Word. I wondered, 'Have I wasted my time coming to this revival?'"[203]

Most Americans are not attuned to the practice of quiet meditative listening. John Ortberg characterizes western society as suffering from "hurry sickness" in which people have become addicted to hurrying. In Ortberg's estimation, hurry has become more than a habit for Americans; it is an addiction. People hurry even when there are no deadlines or time pressures.[204]

As such, Ortberg suggests that people may need the discipline of slowing before they are prepared to wait.[205] To conclude each sermon with an indeterminate period of silent waiting will likely meet with high levels of discomfort and resistance that may negate the spiritual value of the practice. As an intermediate step, the poet-gardener invites the people to experience worship as a time of slowing down and setting aside worries.

---

[203] David Yonggi Cho, *The Fourth Dimension* vol. 2, 120-121.
[204] John Ortberg, *The Life You've Always Wanted*, 111-114.
[205] Ibid.

He or she approaches preaching as a relational event, a time of unhurried conversation among friends. This approach models the discipline of right timing in both the pacing and content of preaching. Utilizing a conversational mode of unhurried speech and narrative framework, the preacher invites the faith community to sit and visit for a time of intimate sharing. In this context, time comes to be viewed as a season of being together with friends rather than an allotted space for an activity. Engagement with the preacher and his or her sermon becomes the venue for waiting together to hear a word from God. In active listening, the congregation engages a process of internal quieting in which one can listen to his or her own thoughts, reactions, and inner longings. Here lies the essence of waiting on God.[206]

Discipline of Doing Things for the Right Reason

"If I give all I possess to the poor and surrender my body to the flames, but have not love, I gain nothing" (1 Corinthians 13:3). In this statement, Paul summarizes a tragic scenario of doing the right things for the wrong reasons. He uses this example of misguided religious actions to set the stage for the call to the discipline of love. Using the word, *agape*, for love, he calls the Church to do all things in God's love, love which overflows from the character of God in self-sacrifice and without regard to the worthiness of the one who is loved.[207] In Pauline terms, agape love is the fundamental right reason for the Christian life.

---

[206] Wendy M. Wright, *Seasons of a Family's Life: Cultivating the Contemplative Spirit at Home* (San Francisco: Jossey-Bass, 2003), 39-40.
[207] F.L. Cross and E.A. Livingstone, ed., *The Oxford Dictionary of the Christian Church* (New York: Oxford University Press, 2005), 928-929.

C.S. Lewis compares the discipline of agape love to gardening. As he explores the metaphor of gardening, he suggests that the homely tasks of the gardener-weeding, watering, hoeing-are necessary but not sufficient for the growth of the garden.

"And when the garden is in its full glory, the gardener's contributions to that glory will still have been paltry compared with those of nature. When he has done all, he has merely encouraged here and discouraged there powers and beauties that have a different source. But his share, though small, is indispensable and laborious."[208]

The poet-gardener knows the laborious nature of disciplined love. Here love rises above a feeling based love (eros) or even love that arises out of a sense of connection or mutual loyalty (philios). Agape love is the discipline of intentionality, taking the risk and the initiative to love people without regard to pay-offs. Drawing again upon Lewis' reflections, preaching is an expression of "gift love," that form of love that overflows from a loving nature with no strings attached. Gift love stands in contrast to need love, loving others because they meet your needs and give you something back.[209]

At a question and answer session with newly ordained United Methodist pastors, Bishop Earl Hunt was asked, "What is the greatest danger to the ministry today?" Bishop Hunt responded without pausing, "Selfish ambition."[210] His comment echoes Paul's concerns about misguided motives for ministry, "Do nothing out of selfish ambition or vain conceit" (Philippians 2:3). Preachers face the constant temptation to use the pulpit ministry for selfish purposes or self-glorification. Agape love is the antidote to such misguided motives. In Paul's terms, "Your attitude should be the same as that of Christ Jesus . . . who emptied himself, taking the very nature of a servant" (Philippians 2: 5, 7).

Discipline of Doing Things in the Right Spirit

---

[208] C.S. Lewis, C.S., *The Four Loves* (New York: Harcourt, Brace and Company, 1960), 164.
[209] Ibid, 11-16.
[210] Earl G. Hunt, "Selfish Ambition," (lecture, Lakeland First United Methodist Church, Lakeland, Florida, May, 1987).

Bruce Larson relates the story of a pastor who was offered the gift of a case of cherry brandy by a parishioner. The gift came with one condition. The pastor had to publicly acknowledge the gift from the pulpit. On the next Sunday, the pastor announced: "I would like to publicly thank Mr. Bruton for his kind gift of a case of cherries and the spirit in which he gave them!"[211] This humorous anecdote makes an important point about doing things in the right spirit. How might one preach in a way that promotes disciplines of right spiritedness and, more specifically, openness to the work of the Holy Spirit?

Twenty-first century preachers address people who are hungry for spirituality. As noted earlier, spirituality has become the term of choice for all things religious. Notwithstanding the popularity of spirituality, it is fraught with murky imprecision. Ken Collins observes that the term, spirituality, is "largely amorphous, lacking definitional precision, often referring vaguely to some interior state or heightened awareness or perhaps to participation in a project, however conceived, greater than oneself."[212]

In a sense, the lack of specificity of spirituality is part of its attraction to postmodern persons. Under the aegis of spiritual orientation, people find freedom to pursue a radically privatized search for meaning without restriction of doctrinal guidelines or moral strictures. Among the many dangers inherent in this individualistic approach is the lack of any moral consensus. Reflecting on this subject, Harvey Cox

---

[211] Bruce Larson, *Luke,* vol. 26 The Preacher's Commentary (Nashville: Thomas Nelson, 2002), 202.
[212] Kenneth J. Collins, *Exploring Christian Spirituality: An Ecumenical Reader* (Grand Rapids: Baker Books, 2000), 10.

characterizes twenty-first century America as a "doughnut-shaped society" with many special interests around the perimeter but lacking a moral center.[213]

The poet-gardener responds to people's hunger for spirituality in ways that resonate with Paul's initial use of the term (pneumatikos, spiritualis). In speaking of the spiritual person (Galatians 6:1), he points to a certain kind of life (life in the Spirit) in contrast to the natural or carnal life. Commenting on this subject, Walter Principe writes: "The spiritual person is one whose life is guided by the Spirit of God; the carnal person is one whose life is opposed to the working and guidance of the Holy Spirit."[214]

In many ways, the great obstacle to doing things in the right spirit is the divided heart. Duplicity and divided interests characterize the human condition. As such, Christians continue to resonate with Paul's anguished autobiographical comment: "We know that the law is spiritual, but I am unspiritual, sold as a slave to sin. I do not understand what I do. For what I want to do, I do not do, but what I hate, I do" (Romans 7:14, 15).

The challenge the poet-gardener faces, then, is to help listeners move beyond popular notions of the spiritual life to seek authentic life in the Spirit. Christian spirituality cannot be reduced to a feel-good, amoral experience of the more than. For Christians, doing things in the right spirit involves following Jesus through the movement of the Holy Spirit. Ortberg speaks of the "well-ordered heart" as the discipline through which one is empowered to follow Christ wholeheartedly.[215]

---

[213] Harvey G. Cox, *The Secular City: Secularization and Urbanization in Theological Perspective* (New York: Collier, 1990), 14.
[214] Walter Principe, "Toward Defining Spirituality," *Exploring Christian Spirituality: An Ecumenical Reader* ed, ed. Kenneth J. Collins (Grand Rapids, MI: Baker Academic, 2000), 45.
[215] John Ortberg, *The Life You've Always Wanted*, 211-212.

Without denying inner spiritual struggle, the poet-gardener calls the congregation to a discipline of wholeheartedness in devotion to God. Wholeheartedness involves self-examination, particularly of the volitional and emotional life, in order to detect ulterior motives, duplicity, and emotional reactivity. In the positive, one embraces a wholehearted life by willingness and earnest desire to serve God. Modern martyr, Jim Elliot, put it plainly: "Wherever you are, be all there."[216]

*The Anatomy of **Dispositions** in Preaching*

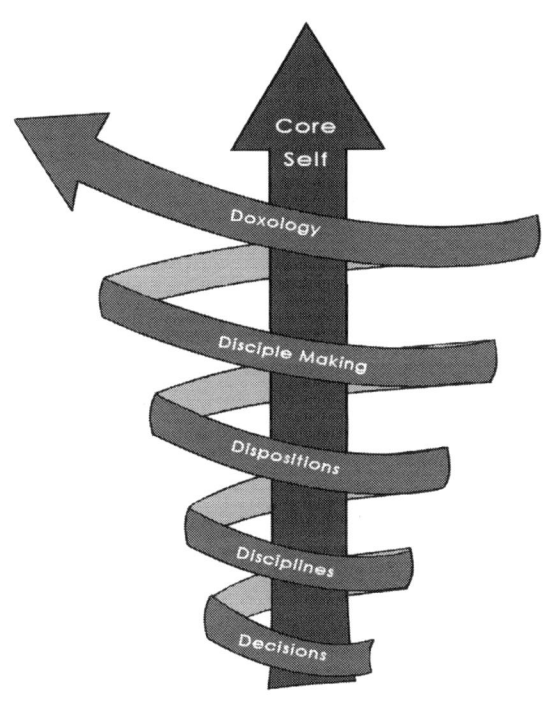

Figure 3-3 The Rhythm of Soul Care

"Woe to you, teachers of the law and Pharisees, you hypocrites! You give a tenth of your spices-mint, dill, and cumin. But you have neglected the more important matters of the law-justice, mercy, and faithfulness. You should have practiced the latter without neglecting the former" (Matthew 23:23). Jesus harshly admonished the religious leaders

---

[216] Elisabeth Elliot, *Shadow of the Almighty: The Life and Testament of Jim Elliot* (New York: HarperOne, 1989), 48.

of his day for making spiritual disciplines the raison d'etre of religion. In their legalistic focus on petty details of religious practice, these people neglected development of a godly disposition marked by qualities such as justice, mercy, and faithfulness.

As stated earlier, disciplines are intentional training toward a higher purpose. That purpose is the formation of a cluster of dispositions that emulate the character of Christ. Herein lies the meaning of transformation (*metamorphoo*). "Do not be conformed any longer to the patterns of this world, but be transformed by the renewing of your mind" (Romans 12:2). Commenting on Paul's use of *metamorphoo*, W.E. Vine observes that the term suggests one might "undergo a complete change which, under the power of God, will find expression in character and conduct; *morphe* (root word) lays stress on the inward change." Further, Vine observes that the present continuous tense of *metamorphoo* implies an ongoing process of change rather than a sudden, dramatic event.[217]

From the perspective of human development, dispositions are viewed as personality traits with roots in both neurological heredity and learned behavior. Beyond these generalized assumptions, psychologists disagree significantly as to the operative dynamics at work in dispositional formation. In their research with monozygotic twins, Clark and Grunstein suggest that personality traits are "hard wired." In other words, their research suggests that people are born with a durable, unchanging temperament or disposition.[218]

On the other hand, behavioral psychologists reduce dispositional traits to nothing more than over-learned habits. In their view, humans develop default settings or

---

[217] W.E.Vine, *Vine's Expository Dictionary of New Testament Words*, 3339.
[218] William Clark and Michael Grunstein, *Are We Hardwired? The Role of Genes in Human Behavior*. (New York: Oxford Press, 2004), 12-15.

automatic behavior-unreflective, subconscious habits-over time through practice of responses to stimuli. Through the process of habit formation, one develops a lifestyle routine or cluster of automatic behaviors. These automatic behaviors occur so frequently and predictably as to be experienced as "just the way I am." That is, habitual behavior is perceived as the norm. Yerkes and Dodson contribute to the conversation by suggesting that one's dispositions might be characterized as responses of thought, action, and feeling in the face of crisis or anxiety.[219]

The debate among researchers about the nature of human disposition hinges in large part on the question of change. Can a person change his or her disposition or does disposition, that is, one's personality, remain unchanged throughout a lifetime? As noted, social scientists disagree widely on this subject. However, the Biblical witness is clear. The converting power of Christ in human life is holistic, inclusive of all domains of human functioning. "If anyone is in Christ, he is a new creation; the old has gone, the new has come!" (2 Corinthians 5:17). Spiritual transformation is more than a change in degree. It is a change in kind. To be in Christ is to experience this profound level of change in all dimensions of life.[220]

Contrary to assumptions in developmental psychology, the Biblical witness does not suggest that humans might develop a Christ-like disposition through strictly human means. Humans are all created in the image of God, but we are not born with the character of Christ. Moreover, one does not become Christ-like by strict training alone. Paul portrays dispositional formation as fruit of the Holy Spirit that flows out of the life

---

[219] Robert Yerkes and J.D. Dodson, "The relation of strength of stimulus to rapidity of habit-formation," *Journal of Comparative Neurology and Psychology*, 18, 1908, 459-482.
[220] C.K. Barrett, *A Commentary on the Second Epistle to the Corinthians* (Peabody, Massachusetts: Hendrickson, 1987), 124.

of one who is keeping in step with the Spirit (Galatians 5:22-25). To the extent that sermons promote change of dispositions, the preacher depends upon the anointing of the Holy Spirit to empower this transformation.

The *METAMORPH* Soul Care Typology is a model for dispositional formation that integrates a variety of resources from soul care tradition as well as social sciences.[221] The *METAMORPH* model builds upon several key assumptions:

- A "Christ transforming culture" theological orientation. Drawing upon the thinking of Francis Bacon, and much later, Richard Niebuhr, *METAMORPH* affirms that God speaks through two books: the book of God's Word and the book of God's works.[222] The implication here is that God's revelation is not limited to the Bible; humans draw wisdom from the created order as well. *METAMORPH* model operates on the hierarchical assumption that the Scriptures serve as the interpretive grid for all other means of human knowledge. In other words, God is revealing God's reconciling love in many ways throughout the world. The challenge is to faithfully interpret God's activity in the world.

- Meta-theoretical eclecticism. *METAMORPH* is an intentionally eclectic model of soul care, drawing upon sources from theology, spirituality, and psychology. As Jones and Butman point out, Christian thinkers must approach theoretical eclecticism with a sensitivity to the moral dimensions at stake. In the absence of a morally sensitive, coherent meta-theory, even well-meaning and well trained

---

[221] Brewer, Guy R., "METAMORPH Integrative Christian Counseling Grid," (lecture, Anderson University School of Theology, September, 2005).
[222] Francis Bacon, Francis *The Advancement of Learning fifth edition,* trans. William Aldis Wright (Oxford: Clarendon, 1926), 37.

preachers may find themselves in error in assuming that "what they do works."[223]

- As a meta-theory, *METAMORPH* relies upon insights into human functioning that come from spiritual formation and soul care tradition. Psychological insights are important. And yet, *METAMORPH* acknowledges that many psychological constructs rely upon a humanistic anthropology that contradicts Biblical worldview. As such, a meta-theory grounded in Christian tradition ensures that the preacher uses psychological resources in a responsible way.

- Redemptive view of humanity. *METAMORPH* affirms that no one is beyond redemption and that soul care is fundamentally a redemptive process. The point of soul care is reconciliation and restoration of the person with Jesus Christ. Through restoration of one's relationship with God, real transformation becomes a possibility. Soul care goes beyond incremental change or even success in worldly terms to hold out hope for a qualitative change in life through the power of the Holy Spirit.

- Holistic functioning. *METAMORPH* maps human functioning into nine domains that cover the span of human functioning. No area of human functioning is more important than another. Equally, the domains identified in *METAMORPH* are not static, self-contained components of human life. Rather, a fundamental assumption of holistic approaches is that the whole of the person is greater than

---

[223] Stanton L. Jones and Richard E. Butman, *A Comprehensive Christian Appraisal of: Modern Psychotherapies* (Downers Grove, Illinois: InterVarsity Press, 1991), 390.

229 Eugene H. Peterson, *Christ Plays in Ten Thousand Places: A Conversation in Spiritual Theology*, 27.

the sum of the parts. The poet-gardener acknowledges that he or she cannot appeal to the mind without touching emotions or will.

- Inside-out dynamics of change. *METAMORPH* affirms the insight of soul care tradition that lasting change, and especially transformation of character, occurs through a change of heart, that is, the core self. As such, transformation is always an "inside job." The focus for the preacher is heart level change.

- Servanthood. The purpose of the *METAMORPH* model is to serve the needs of others. *METAMORPH* is simply a tool to promote intentionality in loving others as whole persons.

- Humility. *METAMORPH* assumes that all healing comes from God and that the Holy Spirit provides wisdom for life-changing preaching. This model also insists that the integrity of the preacher, including self-awareness of limitations and sinfulness, is a key dynamic.

Table 3-5 illustrates the *METAMORPH* Soul Care Typology. The typology builds upon the Pauline notion of "new creation," a state of being in which God has transformed those who are "in Christ" (2 Corinthians 5:17). To be a new creation represents a conversion of dispositions from carnal attitudes of the heart to Christ-like dispositions.[224] *METAMORPH* suggests that the lived pattern of new creation emerges over time through practice of disciplines that lead to godly dispositions.

---

[230] Kenneth L. Chafin, *The Communicator's Commentary: First and Second Corinthians* (Nashville: Word Publishing Group, 1985), 168.

Table 3-5 METAMORPH Soul Care Typology

Domain	Carnal Disposition	Christ-like Disposition	Spiritual Discipline(s)
Mind	Faulty images of God, others, and self	Wisdom	Formative study and meditation on Scripture
Emotions	Impulsivity, anxiety, insensitivity	Peacefulness, Self-control, compassion	Redemptive suffering, bearing one another's burdens
Transformative Goals	Self-absorption, Idolatry of power, possessions, prestige	Fear of the LORD	Obedience, Worship
Actions	Indulgence of flesh and sinful desires	Godly lifestyle	Accountability, Confession
Motivation	Selfish goals, ulterior motives	Love of God and neighbor	Self-examination
Organic Life	Self-indulgence, lack of stewardship of body	Sacred rhythm of life that treats body as temple of the Holy Spirit	Self-denial, fasting, self-care practices
Relationships	"Need Love"-Using others to meet your needs	Gracefulness and faithfulness in relationships	Servanthood to others
Pneumatic Factors	Functional, counterfeit spirituality	Spirit-filled life	Prayer, solitude, and worship
History	Bitterness, deep woundedness from past	Wounded Healer	Forgiveness

Finding the Heart's True Home

To form Christ-like dispositions is more a return to the original pattern of human life than an innovation. It is a homecoming, finding the heart's true home. But as Gerald May comments, "Homecoming is only the beginning of homemaking."[225] In this metaphor, May suggests that the conversion event (homecoming) must be accompanied by a conversion process (homemaking) that involves a transformation over time of one's

---

[225] Gerald May, *Addiction and Grace*, 147.

deepest loyalties or attachments. The term "attachment" is a synonym for treasure. Jesus asserts that discovering our true treasure reveals the true heart or dispositions of a person. "For where your treasure is, there your heart will be also" (Matthew 6:21).

If the preacher is to address attachments and dispositions, he or she must work with the depth dimension of human experience. Many sermons focus on reformation of behavior, limiting the aim of the preacher to change at a behavioral level. The poet-gardener understands that dispositional level change requires a transformation of desire, that is, different attachments or treasures in the person's life. To facilitate dispositional change, sermons must go beyond obvious, outward appearances to motivations of the heart that underlie behavior.

Freedom in the spirit is a dispositional marker for the work of the Holy Spirit. "Where the Spirit of the LORD is, there is freedom" (2 Corinthians 3:17). Authentic freedom requires deliverance from the bondage of attachment to persons and things other than God. Ironically, the Biblical witness suggests that people resist freedom at the same time they long for it.

Jesus stated, "The truth will set you free" (John 8:32). And yet, his audience denied the need to be set free. "We have never been slaves to anyone. How can you say that we shall be set free?" (John 8:33). These people were stuck in the bondage of denial and rebellion to God. The poet-gardener helps people go beyond denial of bondage to admit their need for deliverance.

And, the preacher exhorts his or her listeners to take a risk to go beyond the familiar and controllable. Outside of Christ, human effort is devoted to controlling and managing one's self and one's circumstances. If one is to experience a change of heart or disposition, he or she must let go of the need to be in charge and trust God. For change of heart, one must surrender his or her agenda to God, seeking to desire what God desires.

Finally, the preacher must be aware of the human tendency to co-opt grace for one's own selfish purposes, twisting the Word of God to validate personal desires. The temptation is to convert the gospel into a self-help program that supports my agenda. A change of dispositions requires a submissive spirit that waits on God's timing and way.[226]

One of the great challenges to developing Christ-like dispositions is the pain of change. Inevitably, the desert experience awaits those who seek authentic transformation. Of course, the desert can take many forms-a sense of dryness, deprivation, despondency, feeling all alone. Left to one's own devices, few would endure the desert for long. And yet, the desert is the experience of suffering that produces perseverance, character, and hope (Romans 5: 3-5).

Herein lies the great challenge of preaching. The preacher must enter the desert ahead of her or his people. Soul care preaching requires a willingness to suffer the agony of change as a prerequisite to calling others to heart level change. And, the preacher must be willing to remain in the desert to accompany his or her people. Sunday morning can feel like forty years of wandering in Sinai.

The desert journey begins in confronting the comfort myth, that is, the notion that life ought be comfortable and that something is wrong if one is uncomfortable. In order to facilitate dispositional change, the preacher must be willing to address uncomfortable topics. He or she must risk the displeasure of the congregation and be willing to redundantly address subjects that others would rather not discuss. Such preaching

---

[226] Gerald May, *Addiction and Grace*, 47-48.

requires faith to stand without affirmation or validation from the people relying upon the assurance that God is under girding one's efforts.

Anyone who lives in the desert knows the meaning of thirst. Dispositional change involves a heightened sense of thirst for God. That is to say, one experiences a longing for deepening relationship and knowledge of God. Soul care preaching embodies the paradox of Jesus' beatitude, "Blessed are those who hunger and thirst for righteousness for they will be filled" (Matthew 5:6). The preacher's role is two-fold: To increase the thirst of listeners and to point the way to the well.

Martha Stewart has built a financial empire by offering people tips and techniques for homemaking. However, preaching that helps people make their home in God cannot be reduced to techniques. Techniques offer the allure of control and quick payoffs. The preacher cannot fully know, let alone control, the heart of another person. And, authentic evidence of dispositional change cannot be known in the short-run.
Change of heart or dispositions must be demonstrated over the long haul with perseverance in relationships and through circumstances. Week in and week out the poet-gardener preaches in an active attempt to embrace the facts of grace. What are these facts of grace? Grace is living life as a gift that comes from God in total freedom. Humans cannot determine the timing or parameters of the gift; all one can do is receive the gift. Listeners are invited to become the kind of persons they might yet be in the grace of God. The homecoming becomes homemaking.

*The Anatomy of **Disciple-Making** in Preaching*

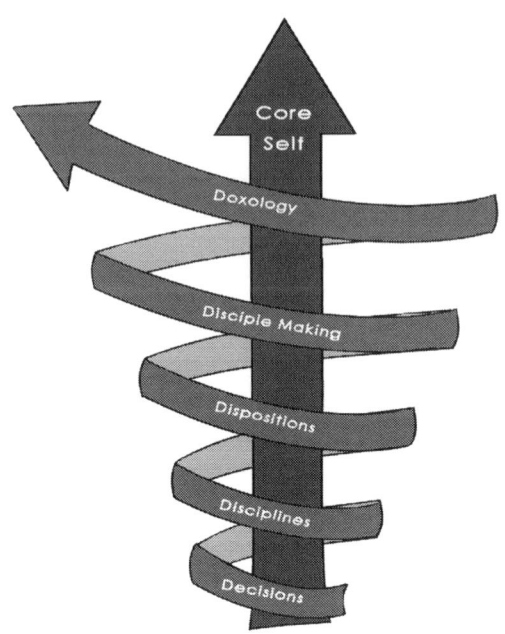

Figure 3-3 The Rhythm of Soul Care

In the spring of 1995 I was visiting with my oldest son, an engineering student at Northwestern university, while he was enjoying spring break. "Tell me about something new you are learning," I prompted. He began talking excitedly about a lecture in which one of his professors described a new technology innovation, the world-wide web. In less than twenty years, the world-wide web and internet have become global influences in the lives of people.

The influence has been more than speed of communication or accessibility to information. These innovations are reshaping people's understanding of propinquity or social networking. Specifically, propinquity refers to elements of proximity, that is, the necessary ingredients of interpersonal interaction.[227] Prior to the internet, propinquity required spatial proximity; people developed relationships because they lived close to one another. With the dawn of electronic connectivity, propinquity can be achieved from remote locations as people share cyber-space. The explosion of social networking sites such as Facebook and Twitter witnesses to the way in which millions of people have embraced electronic connectivity as a legitimate form of propinquity.[228] In other words, to be connected online is perceived as a real connection, no less valuable than talking in person. Without a doubt, people in the twenty-first century are seeing a new way of building relationships.

What are the implications of these shifts in relational dynamics for preaching? In an internet age, no one has the corner on information. People no longer need to turn to the preacher for facts and figures of the Bible or any other subject. Vast amounts of information are just a click away. And, physical proximity has taken on new meaning. The fact that people attend the same church and hear the same sermon does not create the same level of bond that existed prior to the internet. Authentic relationships require something more than sitting elbow to elbow. They require an inner propinquity of shared love, common faith, and unified vision. Preaching must proceed from and promote a web of relationships, a community life that mirrors the first century church. "All the believers were one in heart and mind" (Acts 4:32).

Since the poet-gardener preaches within a web of relationships, sermons are always words of relational connection intended to foster deeper love of God and deeper

---

[227]L. Festinger, S. Schachter, and K. Back, "The Spatial Ecology of Group Formation" in *Social Pressure in Informal Groups* (Palo Alto, CA: Stanford University Press, 1950), Chapter 4.

[228] Felipe Korzenny, "A Theory of Electronic Propinquity: Mediated Communication in Organizations," *Communication Research,* vol. 5, no.1, January 1978, 3-24

love within the faith community. In this sense, preaching is obedience to Jesus' command. "A new command I give you: Love one another. As I have loved you, so you must love one another. By this all men will know that you are my disciples, if you love one another" (John 13:34). Here Jesus clarifies the connection between mutual love and disciple-making. The lived expression of Christian vocation is disciple making- sharing Jesus' love within the faith community and then with others in one's circle of influence. Jesus' teaching points to an organic, relational web of relationships among persons as the evidence of authentic discipleship.

To define one's vocation as disciple making contrasts sharply with prevailing notions. In popular parlance, vocation means job or what one does for a living. One's calling in life is reduced to activity and work. Within the church, disciple-making is often equated with recruiting people to come to church or sponsoring an outreach program to non-Christians. A key task of the poet-gardener is to empower the faith community to claim its vocation of disciple-making.

James A. Fowler contends that misguided notions of human vocation as activity and human effort are endemic within the church. "Evangelical humanism predominates in western churches today. The message is: We can do it. It is up to us. Do your best, give it your all. Be involved, committed, dedicated, and active. Evangelical humanism has already accepted the basic tenets of cosmic humanism-the inherent ability of an alleged independent man to be his own center of reference and the cause of his own effects."[229]

As an alternative vision, the poet-gardener proposes that one's life purpose is more a matter of relationships than individual accomplishment. As those created in the

---

[229] Felipe Korzenny, "A Theory of Electronic Propinquity: Mediated Communication in Organizations," *Communication Research,* vol. 5, no.1, January 1978, 3-24.

image of God, humans find fulfillment and completion in sharing life with others. Figure 3-5 labeled "Web of Discipleship" details the relationship network that under girds Christian vocation. This diagram suggests that discipleship to Christ is more a "we" thing than a "me" thing. Within this web of relationships, each person engages in a mutual exchange of love in various forms that shapes who the person is in Christ.

In a web of discipleship, there are no lone rangers, individual followers of Jesus developing faith on their own. Each person experiences discipleship through belonging to the Body of Christ. The overlapping circles in Figure 3-6 illustrate the shared nature of spiritual life; members of the body are inextricably tied to each other and the life of the body as a whole. The individual circles on the periphery represent five essential types of relationship that facilitate spiritual growth. Their common nexus, the center circle labeled, "personhood," suggests that one discovers and develops human identity through these vital relationships.

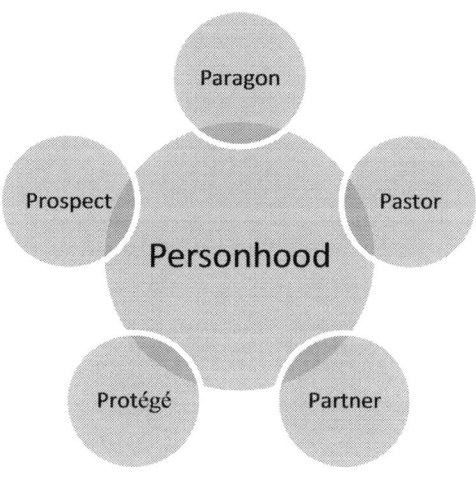

Figure 3-6 Web of Discipleship

"It takes a whole village to raise a child."[230] In this quote, Chinua Achebe points to the fact that humans require a web of relationships in order to grow and mature. Specifically, the poet-gardener model suggests that faith development entails a web of five types of relationships:

1. *Paragon.* A paragon is an exemplar or role model in faith. Jesus serves as the prototype for all disciples. Even so, disciples also require human role models who exemplify the character of Christ.
2. *Pastor.* Disciples require guidance, protection, admonishment, and nurture. Of course, a person may find a pastoral relationship with a minister, but ordination is not a prerequisite. The pastor is a person of greater maturity and genuine love who serves as a wise friend.
3. *Partner.* As Barnabas was to Paul, partner relationships are peer ministry. Disciples need partnerships in which they can receive encouragement, share friendship, and confidentially confess their sins.
4. *Protégé.* To empower a deepening of faith and understanding, the disciple undertakes responsibility for the faith development of a protégé. In this type of relationship, the disciple serves as a mentor to another, taking the role of the wise friend who teaches and models faith.
5. *Prospect.* A key mark of deepening discipleship is sharing the compassion of Christ for persons outside Christian faith. The disciple exhibits the heart of Christ by developing relationships with prospective believers through prayer, patience, and personal investment.

How does the poet-gardener preach within the context of this web of discipleship? He or she is personally embedded in the web, intentionally building relationships as a key part of his or her own discipleship. This means that the preacher places a priority on developing and maintaining the variety of relationships that comprise the web.

In my first parish assignment, I served a three-point charge of rural United Methodist churches. In this parish, I preached twice a month at each church. When I would arrive for services, the people always greeted me warmly, but there was a sense that I was the outsider, the itinerant preacher who showed up from time to time to deliver a sermon. The poet-gardener never preaches as a person isolated from the community.

---

[230] Chinua Achebe, *Things Fall Apart* (New York: Anchor Books), 1994, 2.

The web of discipleship is relational, not spatial. When he or she speaks, the voice is "we" not "I."

As one who is part of a web of discipleship, the poet-gardener not only receives strength and wisdom from the community, but also seeks to enhance the relational connectivity within the faith community. At the same time sermons are applicable to the lives and needs of individuals, they equally point people back to the community as the context in which God's grace is experienced. The consistent emphasis in preaching is the shared quality of faith. Paul uses body imagery to elucidate this truth: "From him (Christ) the whole body, joined and held together by every supporting ligament, grows and builds itself up in love, as each part does its work" (Ephesians 4:16).

Personhood: The Core of the Web of Discipleship

The poet-gardener model envisions discipleship to Christ as tantamount to fulfillment of human personhood as God intended. Hence, Figure 3-5, Web of discipleship, places personhood at the center. This image implies that preaching helps people to discover their personhood through the formation of godly relationships.

In examining the origins of the word, "person," Dennis Kinlaw suggests that the term was theological in its original use. The church fathers (notably Athanasius) employed person as language to symbolize the character of God expressed in the diversity of Father, Son, and Holy Spirit. Contrary to modern assumptions, the application of person to humans is a secondary usage, not the primary meaning. Kinlaw writes, "Jesus is the prototypical person in relation to whom all other persons are simply ectypes or analogues of a prototype, Jesus the Son."[231]

---

[231] Dennis F. Kinlaw, *Let's Start with Jesus: A New Way of Doing Theology* (Grand Rapids: Zondervan, 2005), 78-82.

Drawing upon the doctrine of imago Dei, Kinlaw asserts that humans in their essence are images of another person; one is neither complete nor self-explanatory within himself or herself. As the Creator observes, "It is not good for man to be alone" (Genesis 2:18), God affirms the fundamental connectivity of human life. Each person needs another to complete his or her personhood.[232]

In the context of the Johannine portrait of Jesus, Kinlaw identifies seven prototypical qualities of personhood:

- To be a person is to be conscious of one's identity. Jesus knew who he was.
- Personhood is created and formed through reciprocal relationships.
- Persons find purpose and fulfillment in a web of relationships.
- Persons are created to be free.
- Persons are created with a moral consciousness.
- Personhood involves qualities of openness to others; no man is an island unto himself.
- Persons are not complete in themselves.[233]

Given the fact that the poet-gardener preaches to listeners bathed in postmodern notions of the independent self, what are the implications of personhood for preaching? The psychological understanding of self emphasizes autonomy, self-mastery, and self-actualization. These fundamental assumptions are polar opposites of Jesus' understanding of personhood. The need to confront individualistic world view and self-centeredness seems obvious. And yet, confrontation alone is an inadequate approach. People cling tightly to self-centeredness out of anxiety, the perceived need to take care of one's self. In the face of alienation and fearfulness, logical arguments against self-centeredness fall on deaf ears.

Jed Brewer, missionary with Mission USA, an evangelistic ministry to gang members and ex-convicts in Chicago, wrote about his preaching ministry at a drug and

---

[232] Dennis F. Kinlaw, *Let's Start with Jesus: A New Way of Doing Theology*, 85-86.
[233] Ibid, 78-101.

alcohol rehabilitation center. The small crowd of listeners included men and women who were sober less than a week, trying to escape the horrors of addiction but uncertain about the journey in which they were engaged. He concluded his sermon to them by saying, "Welcome to your real life. Welcome to God's plan for you. Welcome home!"[234] In this sermon, Jed extends hospitality to his listeners as the first step of discipleship. He makes no attempt to argue with them about the pros and cons of their decision to get sober. Rather, he assures them that they are part of a web of relationships. The life transformation they are seeking is more a homecoming than a solo adventure into unknown territory.

Gabriel Marcel makes the ironic claim that personhood development is hetero-centric (other-centered) rather than heauto-centric (self-centered). Contrary to psychological models that portray the self as an autonomous human core, he proposes that human life is one of "intersubjectivity": "We can understand ourselves by starting from the other, or from others, and only by starting from them."[235]

Here is a key dynamic for the poet-gardener. In preaching, one helps the listener take a next step of discovering his or her personhood. And yet, discovering one's deepest identity is more than a matter of "navel gazing," focusing on one's inner thoughts and feelings in a solitary practice. Rather, poet-gardener preaching invites people to affirm their interconnectedness in the Body of Christ as the defining and refining context of personhood. "I am because we are; we are because I am."[236]

***Paragon*: The Need for a Spiritual Role Model**

---

[234] Jed Brewer, Jed, "Welcome Home," *Mission USA Productions Newsletter*. June, 2009, http://www.missionusa.org, (accessed June 21, 2009).
239 Gabriel Marcel, *The Mystery of Being: Faith and Reality, vol.2* (New York: Lanham, 1951).
240. David G. Benner, *Care of Souls,* 101.

"Let us fix our eyes on Jesus, the author and perfecter of our faith" (Hebrews 12:2). In this exhortation the writer of Hebrews holds up Jesus as the paragon of faith within the web of discipleship. Discipleship is the lived response to Jesus' command, "Follow me" (Matthew 4:19). W.E. Vine suggests that *akoloutheo*, translated "follow," means "union, likeness, one going in the same way."[237] In other words, following Jesus is more than mimicking the words and actions of Jesus; it is becoming the kind of person Jesus is. In the example of Jesus, God has provided a particularity of meaning to the spiritual life. In other words, humans do not define what it means to be a spiritual person. God has provided a fully developed paragon in Jesus. Eugene Peterson comments: "Jesus is the name that keeps us attentive to the God-defined, God-revealed life. His is the name that counters the abstraction that plagues spirituality.'"[238]

Jesus is the paragon of faith, but he is not the only role model. The great challenge of the preacher is to be a person in whom others see Christ. When Paul writes, "Whatever you have learned or received or heard from me, or seen in me-put it into practice" (Philippians 4:9), he takes the courageous step of being a role model in faith. Paul could dare to make this invitation because of his devotion to the principle of living "in Christ." For Paul, evidence of the Christian life lies in the ability of others to see one's life in Christ by seeing Christ in the character of the believer.[239]

If he or she is to be believable, the poet-gardener must join Paul in preaching with confidence that God is present in his or her life. This is to say that the preacher conceives

---

[237] W.E.Vine, *Expository Dictionary of Old and New Testament Words*, 190.
[238] Eugene H. Peterson, *Christ Plays in Ten Thousand Places: A Conversation in Spiritual Theology*, 101.
23 Fred B. Craddock, *Philippians,* Interpretation Bible Commentary for Teaching and Preaching (Louisville: Westminster John Knox, 1985), 72-75.

of sermons as incarnational expressions of the person of Jesus through human personality. The notion of presence in the pulpit entails both the authentic presence of the preacher and the incarnational presence of Christ.

Spiritual presence in the pulpit arises out of a lifestyle of discipleship. The poet-gardener preaches out of his or her encounter with God; the words overflow from the heart. The sermon becomes a lived reality of the Word becoming flesh and dwelling in the life and words of the preacher. When one delivers a sermon, he or she speaks a word from God beyond the words of the preacher.

To build a web of discipleship requires an awareness that listeners have been shaped for good or ill by a variety of role models. The preacher must not only point people to paragons of faith. He or she must also confront deformative role models. In my teenage years, my father frequently admonished me: "Take a good look at your friends because you're most likely going to become just like them." The common sense wisdom of my father's advice is good counsel for the poet-gardener.

Outside of Christ, humans rely solely on human role models as patterns of how to live. Of course, all human role models are a mix of virtues and vices. In his analysis of human development, Heinz Kohut suggests that role modeling is the driving engine of self-image. His self-psychology research points to a process of transference in which people acquire the attributes of persons of influence around them on conscious and unconscious levels.[240]

Poet-gardener preaching trains listeners to bring this transference process to a conscious level. He or she invites the faith community to be more attentive to the details

---

[240] Heinz Kohut, *The Analysis of the Self* (New York: International Universities Press, 1971), 121-146.

of character in role models. Secular culture is dominated by a celebrity mindset in which persons in the limelight are idolized with little discrimination about the character of the person. The preacher invites star-struck listeners to look beyond the glittering surface of celebrity image and carefully re-examine their role models. How does your role model exhibit the character traits of Jesus? Does this person exhibit a lived pattern of faithfulness and fruitfulness over a lifetime?

Pastor: The Shepherd's Perspective

Horatio Spafford composed the beloved hymn, *It Is Well With My Soul,* in 1873 as a prayer in the midst of crushing grief. Two years earlier, his only son had died. In that same year, the great Chicago fire destroyed Spafford's home and business, leaving him in financial ruin. Then, in 1873 all of his surviving children, four daughters, drowned in a shipwreck while in route with their mother to Europe. Compelled by these terrible circumstances to sail to England to meet his wife, Spafford's ship passed over the very spot where his daughters had perished. In response to his deep sorrow, he penned *It Is Well With My Soul,* a prayer and personal testimony of resilient hope springing from steadfast faith.[241]

Countless people have drawn inspiration from *It Is Well With My Soul,* particularly in times of loss. Horatio Spafford's story inspires one, but it also raises profound questions for pastoral care and preaching. How does the preacher serve as a pastor to people in the face of their suffering? Specifically, how does the poet-gardener model of preaching entail elements of pastoral preaching?

---

246 Rachael Phillips, *It Is Well With My Soul: Four Dramatic Stories of Great Hymn Writers* (Uhrichsville, OH: Barbour, 2004), 14-30.

In an ironic sense, the preacher would have an advantage in soul care of persons like Horatio Spafford. His circumstances were horrific. And yet, his devastating losses were also public, described in detail in the newspaper. The faith community could not restore Spafford's lost children, but they could stand with him in the solidarity of their loving concern and prayers. Without violating anyone's confidence, the preacher knew enough of Spafford's suffering to speak directly to his needs and to rally the people to support him in specific ways.

Much of the time, the preacher faces a congregation in which people's suffering is hidden or obscured. The poet-gardener preaches from a posture of compassion for the suffering of others and with the confidence that no circumstances lie beyond the healing and redemptive power of the Gospel. As she or he stands with people in their suffering, the preacher takes them seriously and avoids discounting the depth of their anguish with premature, triumphal sermons. And yet, the poet-gardener also claims the Biblical promise that God works through faith to convert suffering from a problem to potential for new life in Christ. "And we know that in all things God works for the good of those who love him, who have been called according to his purpose" (Romans 8:28).

Henri Nouwen draws upon the image of the Grand Canyon to reflect upon the role of suffering or woundedness in preaching. On the one hand, the Grand Canyon is a deep wound in the earth. But it is also a source of incredible beauty and joy to all who behold it. As a metaphor for the spiritual life, he suggests that our wounds embody both deep suffering and profound potential for blessing. In his model, preaching involves a transformation of life's wounds into a source of healing.[242]

---

[242] Henri Nouwen, *The Wounded Healer*, 14-15.

Poet-gardener preaching begins at the point of people's woundedness. This is not to suggest that soul care in any form, let alone preaching, offers a quick fix. More than offering answers to life's dilemmas, the poet-gardener seeks to accompany suffering people with the faith that God is present in their solidarity. The process of accompaniment is complicated enough when ministering to individuals in personal conversation. It is exponentially more complex in the act of preaching to a congregation. Here the struggles of listeners are many, varied, and often hidden from the knowledge of the preacher. Gregory the Great offers the caution that soul care preaching must exhort in a way that "Virtues are fostered in each without encouraging the growth of vices opposed to such virtues."[243]

In further comment on the subject, Gregory compares soul care through preaching to the sport of wrestling, "Deftly dodging this move and that ploy while trying to get in a telling move at exactly the right time."[244] Here the poet-gardener feels some kinship to Jacob as he wrestles with God in his quest for faith. Authentic faith involves a process of struggle and testing.

For many people, a first act of soul care in this cosmic wrestling match is to offer assurance that struggle is normative in the journey of faith. On the heels of misguided evangelical zeal, many Christians have been taught that doubts and struggles are evidence of a lack of faith in God. Soul care preaching gives folks permission to take God to the mat as they wrestle with the anguish of their lives and questions about God's role in their struggles. Permission giving can be the beginning of a restorative process for many.

---

[243] Gregory the Great, *Pastoral Care*, 336.
[244] Ibid.

Building upon the analogy of wrestling, what are other qualities of poet-gardener preaching that support a congregation in struggling through difficult circumstances to a victory in faith? Great wrestlers have an uncommon combination of agility, strength, endurance, flexibility, pace or timing, and passion. Soul care preaching equally requires a cocktail of these qualities. The ability to flexibly interact with the responses and nuances of the listeners must he held in balance with unwavering commitment to the gospel and steadfast love of the people.

Perhaps the most difficult maneuvers in soul care preaching involve issues of timing. Gregory suggests that every congregation includes persons suffering from extremes in responding to God's timing.[245] Some are precipitous and impulsive, running ahead of God in their hurriedness and urgency addiction. Others are overly timid, frozen in their fear of failure and condemnation. Both forms of excess betray a deep inner anxiety. Soul care preaching engages listeners in these inner life processes by offering the assurance of God's presence that empowers alternative paths in life.

The poet-gardener assures the faith community that God is with us in a particular way. God is more our dance partner than our wrestling opponent. God is not competing for our time and attention. God is calling us to cooperation in life, a cooperation that involves keeping in step with the Spirit.

Since the larger context in which the poet-gardener preaches is his or her role as a pastor, sermons are pastoral communication. J. Randall Nichols offers a definition of pastoral preaching: "Human communication which affects and involves the deeply personal in us and, moreover, which does so to some extent by the design and intention of

---

[245] Gregory the Great, *Pastoral Care,* 35.

the communicator. Finally, what makes preaching pastoral is the impact of the sermon on the listener whether intended by the preacher or supplied by the hearers."[246]

The New Testament uses the same term, *poimen,* "one who tends the flock," to mean shepherd or pastor.[247] How does one preach in a way that is pastoral? Seward Hiltner suggests that one might envision pastoral preaching as a message from the perspective of sacrificial love. The emphasis in preaching is not technical skill or artistic beauty, but sacrificial love for the congregation. Contrary to the negative connotations of the preacher as one who "preaches at" people, a pastoral perspective suggests that sermons are words of healing, a word preached "with" the people.

Hiltner enumerates several critical dimensions to a pastoral perspective in preaching: alertness, readiness to act, incisive timing, flexibility. Taken together, all of these qualities of preaching paint the picture of shepherding that responds to the perceived needs of persons. The poet-gardener diligently studies and prepares to preach but with the knowledge that the pastoral sermon is not set in stone. He or she is preparing more for an interaction with the congregation than an oral presentation. Hiltner observes: "Any attempt to wrap the Gospel in a cellophane package, as if it could be given the same way on all occasions, betrays what is required. The mode of testimony should be according to the need in the situation."[248]

Aden and Hughes identify seven common mistakes that preachers make in pastoral sermons:

---

[246] Randall J. Nichols, *The Restoring Word: Preaching as Pastoral Communication* (New York: Harper and Row, 1987), 13-15.
[247] W.E.Vine, *Expository Dictionary of Old and New Testament Words*, 2005, 4166.
[248] Seward Hiltner, "The Solicitous Shepherd," in *Images of Pastoral Carr: Classic Readings,* ed. Robert Dykstra (St. Louis: Chalice Press, 2005), 47-53.

- Using the Bible more as a resource than a source with topic rather than text dominating sermon.
- Offering false hope by claiming that intransigent problems have predictable solutions.
- Relying more on pop psychology than theology or making errors in integration of theology and psychology.
- Using the pulpit as a "confessional booth" and engaging in inappropriate self-disclosure.
- Employing reductionist, moralistic approaches that offer folks "magic potions" or how-to formulae for their problems.
- Preaching a narrow personalism that over focuses on personal issues to the exclusion of community life and social justice issues.
- Over emphasizing Jesus' humanity for purposes of relevance and empathy with a de-emphasis on his divinity.[249]

The poet-gardener must avoid these excesses while fulfilling her or his pastoral role. The goal of the pastoral sermon is to help people make sense of life in the face of circumstances that have assaulted their assumptive world and created an inescapable sense of disequilibrium. Aden and Hughes suggest that pastoral preaching begins with a critical question. "What is God doing here, first in the text, and then in the life situation of this suffering person?"[250] Although the nature and scope of people's problems vary considerably, the poet-gardener keeps certain goals in mind in responding to this question of suffering.

Where pastoral preaching is concerned, a central purpose in proclamation is to give the community and individuals a voice to name their pain and claim their suffering. Many people suffer in silence; the inability to articulate their anguish exacerbates their pain and prevents others from supporting them in healing. To name one's problems is to face reality, a reality in which God is living and active.

---

[249] LeRoy H. Aden and Robert G. Hughes, *Preaching God's Compassion: Comforting Those Who Suffer* (Minneapolis: Fortress Press, 2002), 35-36.
[250] Ibid.

To name suffering is not to solve it. For many if not most, their painful circumstances continue without a definite end in sight. The faith community often joins Isaiah in crying out, "How long, O LORD?" (Isaiah 6:11). As such, pastoral preaching has an important sustaining function to support people who must endure suffering over time. Without minimizing or discounting anyone's suffering, the poet-gardener seeks to lift the vision of the faith community beyond the natural fixation on the immediate, excruciating pain to a larger vision of God's sovereignty, compassion, and loving purposes.[251]

Partner: **Community Dynamics**

When the poet-gardener preaches, she or he engages in "community speak." Speaking as a partner to fellow believers, the preacher gives voice to the shared faith of the community. Even more, he or she speaks out of community with God through the Holy Spirit (John 15:26, 27). The dynamic of a "trialogue" is at work here. Sermons are a three-way partnership involving the shared witness of the Holy Spirit, the preacher, and the faith community.

Jesus' preaching sets the example for trialogue; His claim is that healing and liberation flow out of the trialogue of preaching. In his inaugural sermon at Nazareth, Jesus claimed the anointing of the Holy Spirit in keeping with the prophecy of Isaiah (Isaiah 61:1, 2) and announced, "Today, this scripture is fulfilled in your hearing" (Luke 4:16-21). Jesus' preaching is the embodiment of God's Word living and acting among the people. When he preached, Jesus sought more than cognitive assent to the truths he proclaimed. He called his listeners to a family conversation that would thoroughly

---

[251] LeRoy H. Aden and Robert G. Hughes, *Preaching God's Compassion: Comforting Those Who Suffer,* 51-52.

revolutionize one's life. "I came that you might have life and have it to the full" (John 10:10).[252]

.This concept of partnership builds upon a perichoretic understanding of God's life in the Church. Catherine LaCugna offers the intriguing metaphor of "divine dance" (*perichoreuo*) to picture the nature of relationship of the Father, Son, and Holy Spirit. She further suggests that the divine dance characterizes God's partnership with the faith community through a "dynamic and creative energy, the eternal and perpetual movement, the mutual and reciprocal permeation of each person with and in and through and by the other persons."[253] In light of the metaphor of dance, preaching becomes a form of sacred choreography through which God's people become dance partners with the divine, keeping in step with the rhythm of God's movement. Sermons are "events of relationship" in which the Church experiences a living partnership with God marked by the mutuality and reciprocity that inhere within the Trinity.[254]

When visiting an AME Church some years ago, I was struck by the frequent request of the preacher to the congregation: "People, help me out here." In response to this call for help, the people would respond with verbal affirmation and encouragement, "Preach it! Come on now, preacher! Amen!" African-American sermon heritage recognizes that preaching is a partnership between preacher and congregation. The congregation's role in sermons is different from the preacher's, but equally important.

---

[252] Greg Heisler, *Spirit-led Preaching: The Holy Spirit's Role in Sermon Preparation and Delivery* (Nashville: B and H Publishing Company, 2007), 25-38.
257 Catherine Mowry LaCugna, *God For Us: The Trinity and Christian Life* (San Francisco: HarperCollins, 1991), 271.
258 Graham Buxton, *The Trinity, Creation, and Pastoral Ministry* (Carlisle, PA:Paternoster, 2005), 106.

The "call and response" rhythm of African-American preaching affirms that sermons involve many voices articulating a common faith.[255]

The postmodern climate requires that the preacher be intentional in taking the posture of a partner. Among persons whose worldview is shaped more by postmodern categories than church tradition, the prevailing attitude toward preaching is one of suspicion or outright rejection. To build a sense of partnership, John McClure suggests that preachers might assume the role of hospitable host:

"Rather than protecting turf, (preachers) are asking interpretive questions that situate the interpreter less in the role of protector and more in the role of host. A new spirit of generosity pervades exegetical practice today. Listening to interpretations by those on the margins of the community or strangers is becoming more central to exegetical practice. Collaborative interpretation of the Bible with laity and unchurched persons prior to sermon preparation is increasing."[256]

Protégés: Mentoring from the Pulpit

"And the things you have received from me, pass on to faithful men who will be able to teach others also" (2 Timothy 2:2). In the same way that Paul mentored Timothy to become a young leader who would carry on a faithful witness, the poet-gardener seeks to develop people through preaching. In treating listeners as protégés, the preacher seeks to exert intentional influence in developing the character of persons. Tim Elmore notes that generations of people in Western culture have been raised on a Greek model of mentoring that conceives of protégés as passive learners in a classroom setting. He suggests that effective mentoring of twenty-first century people requires more of a

---

[256] John S. McClure, *Other-Wise Preaching: A Postmodern Ethic for Homiletics* (St. Louis: Chalice, 2001), 14.

Hebrew approach that emphasizes active learning through relationships, experience, and on-the-job training.[257]

In what ways might the poet-gardener be intentional about mentoring dimensions of sermons? He or she preaches with the conviction that the Word of God, not human projects, is the central focus of sermons. In this sense, mentoring is not the primary goal; faithful exposition of the Scriptures is the goal of preaching. Nonetheless, Bryan Chappel is correct when he asserts that sermons without real life application are really "pre-sermons" that specialize in unfinished business.[258] In this comment, Chappel's frame of reference is a classical approach to sermon design that employs the outline method and includes an application movement. He sees application as the logical outcome of Biblical exposition.

The poet-gardener affirms the importance of applicability of the sermon. And yet, preaching entails elements of mentoring throughout the sermon, not simply in the application phase. The focus in soul care preaching is more on a change of heart through deepened relationships than response to a well-developed logical argument. As such, sermons might be conceived as building blocks in a process of maturing relationships. Of course, the Holy Spirit works in timing and ways beyond the control or understanding of the preacher. The role of the preacher as mentor is to faithfully edify, sustain, and guide the faith community over time.

Tim Elmore suggests several metaphors for mentoring that provide vivid images for the work of the preacher.

---

[257] Tim Elmore, *Intentional Influence* (Nashville: Lifeway Press, 2003), 18-20.
[258] Bryan Chappel, *Christ-Centered Preaching: Redeeming the Expository Sermon* (Grand Rapids, MI: Baker Academic, 2004), 246-249.

- Mentoring preachers paint pictures. A picture is worth more than a thousand words, evoking deep emotional and memory responses in listeners.
- Mentoring preachers provide handles. Listeners are trying to make sense of their lives and the place that faith plays. Providing handles gives folks a place to hold on.
- Mentoring preachers provide road maps. Without a map, it is impossible to know the destination or the course of life. Listeners resist being told how to live; they welcome being offered a clear path.
- Mentoring preachers furnish a laboratory for faith. Rather than being told how to think, sermons might offer people a place to experience God and experiment with their ideas about faith.[259]

***Prospects*: Going Outside the Circle**

I met Harry Hoston at Concord Park United Methodist Church in Orlando, Florida in 1979. My home church had burned to the ground, so the folks at Concord Park invited us to worship with them until the church could be rebuilt. Concord Park was a rundown church in a rough part of town. As I was walking into the church, I thought I saw something in the overgrown azalea bushes out front; somebody was living behind the bushes. I looked more carefully and there was a scraggly, homeless man looking back at me. Not knowing what else to say, I said, "Good morning." Harry nodded back, "Good morning . . . Say, man, do you have any spare change? I'm hungry." I fumbled around for change but all I had was two quarters which I gave to Harry. "What's your name, man?" I asked. "Harry-Harry Hoston. "God bless you, Harry," I said as I hurried into church.

Once inside the church, I made a beeline to Pastor Ken Crossman and told him about Harry. Pastor Ken leaped out of his chair." We can't have someone living behind the azalea bushes. I'm going to put a stop to that!"

---

[259] Tim Elmore, *Intentional Influence*, 68-70.

Ken returned a few minutes later with Harry in tow. He gave him coffee and doughnuts and invited him to stay for services. I don't know what else he might have planned to preach, but that morning Ken preached Luke 15: 8-10, the story of the lost coin. He introduced the congregation to Harry and thanked God that a lost coin had been found and that Harry was no longer homeless. Ken challenged us to join the search party. Over the next weeks and months, Ken and members of the church helped Harry get his feet back on the ground. We got him involved in drug rehabilitation, found him a place to live, and eventually a job.

Although sermons are often preached to a group of insiders, the gospel was never intended to be an inside message. As Pastor Ken's message on the parable of the lost coin extended to a man who was spiritually and physically homeless, the poet-gardener reaches out to prospects, those who are outside the camp of faith. Ironically, many persons who are functionally outside the camp are counted as constituents by the Church. Kirk Hadaway estimates that inactive members comprise more than forty percent of church membership roles in mainline denominations.[260] Many persons are lost inside the church.

Prospecting in sermons begins as a posture of expectancy. The preacher expects that the congregation includes persons who "don't get it." They have come in quiet desperation, looking for something more in life. Billy Graham famously uses the image of a "hole in your heart" to suggest the sense of emptiness, that visceral yearning that draws people to God.[261]

---

[260] C. Kirk Hadaway and David A. Roozen, *Rerouting the Protestant Mainstream: Sources of Growth and Opportunities for Change* (Nashville: Abingdon, 1994), 91-98.

[261] Billy Graham, "You Have a Hole in Your Heart," (sermon, Jacksonville, Florida, February, 1999).

Even more, the poet-gardener expects God to do something through the sermon. Through the working of prevenient grace, God draws people who are unsure of their faith to hear the Gospel. The Gospel of John characterizes the drawing power of God as emanating from the person of Jesus: "When I am lifted up from the earth, I will draw all men to myself" (John 12:32). More than convincing people of ideas about Jesus, the core of faith prospecting is introducing people to Jesus.

Myron Augsburger points to several key elements of preaching that connect with prospective believers. He suggests the importance of "vicarious dialogue" in preparation and delivery of sermons. In vicarious dialogue, the preacher anticipates the questions and objections of prospective believers to the message of a text. Here the preacher is not trying to persuade people to his or her point of view. Rather, he or she anticipates the deepest concerns of the listener and works intentionally to show how Jesus responds to those concerns.[262]

In preaching to a weekly crowd of ex-convicts, urban missionary, Jed Brewer, dubs his sermons, "The I Don't Get It Minute." His sermons assume that secular people who are new to Christianity do not understand the "churchy" language that often dominates sermons. To them, it is a foreign language. "The I Don't Get It Minute" is an exercise in translating the truths of the Bible and the orthodox doctrines of the Church into colloquial speech of inner-city Americans.[263]

To connect with prospective believers always requires careful attention to language in the sermon. The preacher cannot assume that listeners know the meaning of

---

[262] Myron S. Augsburger, "Preaching Evangelistically," http://www.christianitytoday.com, 2009, (accessed July 1, 2009).
[263] Jed D. Brewer, "The I Don't Get It Minute" (sermon, The Bridge Ministry, Chicago, IL, July, 2009).

theological terms like grace, forgiveness, or joy. In carefully choosing his or her words, the poet-gardener seeks for the language of the sermon to be a conveyance of experience of God. To the extent that sermons entail every day images and offer a reframing of those images in faith terms, the preacher speaks a common language with prospects.

Of course, the winsomeness of a message relies not only on what is said but how it is said. The poet-gardener remains aware of the tone of the sermon to ensure that she or he preaches in a way that assures and invites the unsure and wary. Augsburger suggests that negative messages that specialize in putting down non-Christian worldview tend to be off-putting. A more invitational approach builds a climate of hopefulness in which the preacher stands as a representative of a welcoming Christ.

Finally, Augsburger emphasizes the need for a variety of approaches in preaching to prospective believers. The consistent goal of preaching is to engender faith. Nonetheless, sermons with evangelistic focus do not always employ the same theme. Augsburger comments:

"All evangelistic preaching aims to bring people to a decision to accept Christ. We make a mistake, however, if we assume that all evangelistic preaching must begin and end on the same note. Christ meets needs in a variety of ways: he's the propitiation for our sins, yes, but he's also the norm for ethics, the Shepherd of sheep, the Bread of Life, the Way, the Truth, and the Life." [264]

In addition to variety of themes, sermons that connect with prospective believers recognize that people have come to hear a sermon for a variety of reasons. Not everyone perceives spiritual need as emptiness. Some are bored. Some are terrified. Some are despairing and numb. People may feel a conscious need; others are engaged in a non-specific search for something different. A key movement in preaching is to help listeners

---

[264] Myron S. Augsburger, "Preaching Evangelistically," http://www.christianitytoday.com, 2009, (accessed July 1, 2009).
269 Ibid.

sharpen and name their sense of need. For many, the door to change is the development of a more precise and acute desire for a different quality of life.[265]

In appealing to prospective believers, the preacher must also account for varied contexts of listeners. In fact, the ebb and flow of life does present regular opportunities to preach for prospective believers with little to no church background. Major holidays (Christmas and Easter), cultural observances, funerals, weddings, and special programs featuring children are all occasions on which prospective believers attend church for cultural or family reasons. The key for the preacher is to exegete the listeners as well as the text to understand something about the motivations and worldview of these persons. To simply give a standard altar call because prospective believers are present is a mechanical approach that is more likely to offend than connect. In a sense, the preacher uses the sermon on such occasions to lay the groundwork for a deeper relationship in which prospective persons leave the sermon thinking, "I'd like to hear more."

*The Anatomy of **Doxology** in Preaching*

"The act of preaching is not instruction, rational discourse, or moral suasion. It is the invitation and permit to practice a life of doxology and obedience which properly orders the ongoing relationship of sovereign and subject, which is seasons of trust like that of parent-child, or even friend and friend (John 15:14-15). The preacher is to enact doxology with and for the congregation."[266]

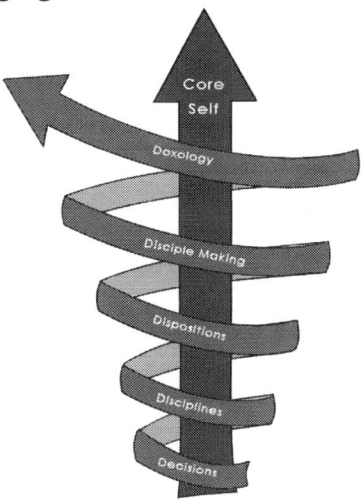

Figure 3-3: Rhythm of Soul Care

The culminating movement in the rhythm of soul care preaching is doxology. This is to say that preaching must ultimately reach beyond human connections and agendas to become a "doxa-logia" or glorifying word to God. John uses the word *doxa* to summarize the character of Jesus. "We have seen his glory (*doxa*) the glory of the One and Only, who came from the Father, full of grace and truth" (John 1:14). W.E. Vine suggests that Biblical use of *doxa* specifically refers to God's character, "the nature and acts of God in self-manifestation, i.e., what He essentially is and does, as exhibited in whatever way he reveals Himself."[267]

In reflecting on ways that preaching is a doxology, Walter Brueggemann characterizes preaching as conversation that builds communion with God. By this he

---

[266] Walter Brueggemann, *Finally Comes the Poet* (Minneapolis: Augsburg Fortress Press, 1989), 68.

[267] W.E. Vine, *The Expository Dictionary of Old and New Testament Words,* 1391.

emphasizes that doxology is more than standing afar and admiring the greatness of God. Rather, when we offer God doxology, we are with God even as God is with us.

In a profound sense, God's communion with humans began at creation with an act of speech. "Let us make man in our image, in our likeness" (Genesis 1:26). And, speech is not only the first act of communion with God; it continues to be the primary way that humans articulate oneness with God. Preaching is, then, a meeting with God which involves conversation, a dialogue between God and humans.[268]

At the same time he names preaching as doxology, Brueggemann bemoans the fact that proclamation is often anything but doxology. He identifies two reductionistic tendencies in preaching that mute the voice of praise. On the one hand, the preacher is tempted to engage in an excess of subjective consciousness. These presuppositions limit the world to individualistic perception and point of view. On a public scale, subjectivism leads to a "managerial" or utilitarian approach. Private subjectivism favors a therapeutic, individualistic interpretation of the gospel. In Brueggemann's words, the subjective pole imagines "there is only me (the exaggerated self) and the world can, therefore, be mobilized around me."[269]

At the other extreme, preaching may exaggerate the objective pole in which God is portrayed as a distant, sovereign God who is disconnected from the pain and suffering of people. In this observation, Brueggemann is not attempting to negate the sovereignty of God. Rather, he is pointing to the misguided tendency in preaching to address the deep suffering of people with the pat answer, "God is in charge; let God sort it out."

---

[268] Walter Brueggemann, *Finally Comes the Poet*, 42-77.
[269] Ibid., 48.

Doxology is a voice of truth that corrects both excessive subjectivism and objectivism. The preacher does the imaginative act of rendering in words the conversation between God and humans, speaking words for both parties. Brueggemann suggests a Biblical pattern to the divine-human conversation that includes three movements.

In the first movement worshippers initiate a dialogue with God as they speak out of pain, need, and protest. One might liken the anguished cry of worshippers to the response of a child to a parent returning from a journey. The child's response begins indignantly, "Where have you been so long?" But then, the child proceeds to express a sense of relief and longing fulfilled, "I've missed you so much-please don't ever leave again."[270]

In the second movement of doxology, God responds to the cry of God's people. Brueggemann characterizes God's response as "life voiced from the other side." The pain of people evokes a powerful, intervening response; God speaks and acts. The divine response comes in a prototypical pattern of parental love. Sometimes, the response is no. In the myopic perception that intense suffering creates, God's response can seem harsh and uncaring. But God's no is never like W.C. Field's famous aphorism, "Go away, boy, you bother me." Rather, God's no is always accompanied by "I will be with you." Even when God's timing and methods are bewildering, God's faithfulness and compassion are certainties.

A third element of divine response to human outcry is found in the Job whirlwind speeches (Job 38-41). The tone of God's comments to Job might be summarized as, "Because I said so." God affirms divine sovereignty and the reliability of God's own

---

[270]Walter Brueggemann, *Finally Comes the Poet*, 51.

character as the solid rock foundations of faith. In response, Job answers God with a doxological statement that affirms God's sovereignty: "I know that you can do all things; no plan of yours can be thwarted" (Job 42:2). Ironically, Job's statement of faith in God's sovereignty comes in the depth of his suffering. Despite his bitter complaints and demands to God, nothing has changed in his circumstances. And yet, everything changes as God speaks. God has closed the distance with Job who now has experienced God first hand. "My ears had heard of you, but now my eyes have seen you" (Job 42:5).[271] Doxology begins from below with human words and evokes God's response from the other side. The third movement of doxology is "glad yielding," the praise of God. Praise happens when people are freed enough to participate in their proper vocation. That vocation is the yielding of life to God. As the preacher works to create a fresh conversation with God, he or she offers the people the opportunity to express freely to God the realities of their lives. And, God's response is one of liberation. Brueggemann summarizes doxology: "As we find our tongues, we find our identity and our vocation."[272]

---

[271] Walter Brueggemann, *Finally Comes the Poet*, 55-57.
[272] Ibid., 77.

MOVEMENT FOUR: IMAGES FOR POET-GARDENER PREACHING

Image One: Incarnational Presence

http://www.youtube.com/watch?v=nEQT1o7Uo4Q&featu

L'Abbé Pierre

Dr. Paul Brand, long term president and teacher at the Christian Medical College in Vellore, India, recounts a visit from his friend, Abbé Pierre. Father Pierre was a French monk renowned for founding Emmaus, a ministry to homeless persons and refugees around the world. Following the custom of the medical college, Dr. Brand invited Abbé Pierre to offer a few minutes of comments during the students' community lunch. Since none of the students spoke French, Abbé Pierre spoke to the students with the aid of a translator. As he became more passionate in his comments about the responsibility of the medical community to the poor, Abbé began to speak faster and faster, making it impossible for the translator to keep up. He continued speaking without translation for the next fifteen minutes. The medical students stopped eating and listened with rapt attention. When Abbé Pierre finished speaking, the students gave him a standing ovation.

Intrigued by the powerful connection that Abbé Pierre had made with the students, Dr. Brand asked one of them, "How did you understand? None of you speaks French." The student replied, "We didn't need a language. We felt the presence of God and the presence of love."[273]

---

[273] Paul Brand and Philip Yancey, *Fearfully and Wonderfully Made* (Grand Rapids, MI: Zondervan, 1997), 54-55.

Abbé Pierre's unscripted sermon to medical students stands as a vivid image of preaching with incarnational presence. Pierre's personal presence communicated with his listeners in a way that transcended language. His message overflowed from the most deeply held convictions and passions of his heart. And, the result was more a spiritual experience than an educational program on the problems of homelessness. With no prior knowledge of Abbé Pierre and the story of his ministry, the students sensed his genuineness and wholehearted commitment. These elements of Pierre's spirit-passion, authenticity, boldness, overflowing love-became venues of God's presence through his personality. The student's comment, "We felt the presence of God and the presence of love," points to an incarnational moment in which God inhabited the lunchroom.

Was Abbé Pierre's incarnational sermon a serendipitous, once in a lifetime epiphany of God's presence or are such preaching moments replicable? The poet-gardener recognizes the irony of incarnational presence: it cannot be achieved as a technique or by trying harder to be genuine in the pulpit. Preaching with incarnational presence is more a spiritual posture than a skill set.

Phillips Brooks wrote of the incarnational quality of presence in sermons. "Preaching is truth speaking through personality."[274] When the desire of the preacher is to be with God's people through the act of proclamation, the Word of God nestled in her or his heart becomes a living truth in the community.

Incarnational presence ought not be confused with communication dynamics e.g. poise, personal confidence, eye contact, and charisma. No doubt, rhetorical qualities of personal presence contribute significantly to interpersonal effectiveness. However, the shadow side of overemphasis on such techniques is a self-consciousness in which

---

[274] Phillips Brooks, *The Joy of Preaching* (Grand Rapids, MI: Kregel, 1989), 29.

sermons may lapse into rhetorical performance to the exclusion of a spontaneous, present moment experience of God's presence.

Sometimes, the greatest moments in sermons come when we least expect them. Incarnational presence is a confluence of genuineness, intimacy, immediacy, and inspiration that irresistibly connects with the deep needs of others. In point of fact, those times of greatest impact may not be smooth or elegant. To remain in the present with people often involves the courage to experience raw moments of uncertainty and unscripted emotion.[275]

The poet-gardener does not fear the unpredictable nature of preaching. Rather, she or he views preaching as an expression of the freedom of the Spirit who moves like the wind. As Jesus observed, "The wind blows wherever it pleases. You hear its sound, but you cannot tell where it comes from or where it is going" (John 3:8). In preaching with presence, the preacher's role is to adjust his or her spiritual sails to catch the wind while keeping a light hand on the rudder.

The poet-gardener acknowledges that he or she cannot orchestrate or intentionally create present moment experiences of God. Rather, sermon preparation works as an immersion process in which the preacher marinates her or his thought life in the Word of God. Incarnational sermons organically emerge from the preacher's walk with God. In *The Practice of the Presence of God,* Brother Lawrence writes: "I walk before God simply, in faith, with humility and with love; and I apply myself diligently to do nothing and think nothing which may displease Him."[276] In keeping with the metaphor

---

[275] Post Modern Preaching, Incarnational Preaching," http://www.postmodernpreaching.net/incarnational.html, p. 1-3, (accessed August 14, 2008).
[276] Brother Lawrence, *The Practice of the Presence of God and the Spiritual Maxims* (New York: Cosimo, 2006), 46

of walking with God, preaching with presence is an act of keeping in step with the Spirit and the way the Holy Spirit is moving.

Preparing the Preacher

Before the poet-gardener can prepare sermons that draw the congregation into the presence of God, she or he must spend time preparing the heart of the preacher. Ironically, the nexus of the preacher's self-preparation is losing oneself, sloughing off self-centered concerns about performance and the reactions of others. The spiritual antidote to self-conscious anxiety in the pulpit is confidence in God's empowering presence. When the preacher feels assured that God inhabits her or his words and is working through them, the preaching moment is one of freedom to be authentic and to be fully present with the people.

In many ways, the poet-gardener seeks to be attentive to God's sacramental presence all around us. Preparing to preach involves honing one's awareness of God's grace in the material and temporal things of life. Through sacramental prayer, incarnational study of the Scriptures, and active attunement to community life the poet-gardener senses the ways in which God is present.

Sacramental Prayer

Martin Buber retells a Hasidic parable about sacramental prayer:

"My grandfather was paralyzed. One day he was asked to tell about something that happened with his teacher-the great Baalschem. Then, he told how the saintly Baalschem used to leap about and dance while he was at prayers. As he went on with the story, my grandfather stood up! He was so carried away that he had to show how the master had done it, and started to caper about and dance. From that moment on he was cured."[277]

---

[277] Martin Buber, *Werke: Zweiter Band Schriften zur Bible. Band 2,* vol. 3. quoted in *Care of Souls,* 71.

In this story, Buber points to the power of sacramental prayer at work. As the grandfather's imaginative remembrance of Baalschem's prayers made them his own, the incarnational healing presence of God in those prayers was re-experienced. Sacramental prayer is far more than words or human expressions. It is a connection with the depth dimension of reality that overcomes the barriers of our fractured, compartmentalized lives to unite with the grace of God.

Richard Foster characterizes sacramental prayer: "Sacramental prayer is incarnational prayer. God in his great wisdom has freely chosen to mediate his life to us through visible realities."[278] Here Foster points to the unity of the material and spiritual life.

With the faith that God is present in all things, the poet-gardener approaches prayer as a posture of expectant watching for the evidence of grace. The poet-gardener engages in sacramental prayer as an act of pastoral care in which she or he reflects on the ways that God is present and active in current events and experiences. Praying in this way is more than petition and intercession for needs. Sacramental prayer is an expression of faith that God is already working in all things.

Sacramental prayer prepares the preacher to name God's presence in the world, or as Mary Catherine Hilkert suggests, to "name grace."[279] The poet-gardener recognizes not only the community's need to hear about God's grace, but more importantly, to experience God's grace first-hand. Having prepared himself or herself in prayer, the poet-gardener is ready to proclaim, "Here is grace under our very noses!"

---

[278] Richard Foster, Richard. *Prayer, Finding the Heart's True Home* (San Francisco: Harper Collins, 1992), 105.

[279] Mary Catherine Hilkert, *Naming Grace: Preaching and the Sacramental Imagination* (New York: Continuum, 1998), 44-57.

Incarnational Study of the Scriptures

David Yonggi Cho suggests that incarnational study of the Scriptures involves a spiritual dynamic in which the logos, God's Word to all humanity, become a rhema, God's personal, living Word to a given person.[280] Such an experience of the Word may come as a surprise, but it often comes through forms of study beyond analytical exegesis. The ancient practice of Lectio Divina provides the methodology for ruminating on the Scriptures as a pathway for incarnational moments.

Susan Muto characterizes Lectio Divina as formative reading in contrast to informative reading. Suggesting that formative reading is less like reading a textbook and more like enjoying a letter from a friend, Muto stresses the connection with God that comes from abiding in the Word.[281] As the preacher dwells in the Scriptures, he or she is following Paul's admonishment: "Let the word of Christ dwell in you richly as you teach and admonish one another with all wisdom" (Colossians 3:16). In this reference to dwelling (*enoikeo*), Paul paints a word picture of life shared with God. Literally translated, *enoikeo* is "pitching one's tent" in the camp of friends.[282] Here is the heart of study and sermon preparation for preaching with presence: dwelling in the Word until the Word dwells in the preacher.

Certainly, the poet-gardener engages in serious exegesis and analytical study of the Bible. And yet, cognitive, critical engagement with the Scriptures is far from the totality of sermon preparation. Preaching with presence requires dwelling in the text until it becomes the frame of reference for the preacher's thought life for the week. Dwelling

---

[280] David Yonggi Cho, *The Fourth Dimension,* p. 74-75.
[281] Susan Muto, *Pathways of Spiritual Living* (Pittsburgh: Epiphany Books, 2006), 23-27.
[282] Spiro Zodhiates, *The Complete Word Study Dictionary of the New Testament* (Chattanooga, TN: AMG Publishers, 1992), 592.

in the text might be described as a sacramental pattern in which the preacher's study, prayer life, and interactions in the community merge to become a lens for discerning material evidence of God's presence in the world.

The operative word here is "pattern." Incarnational study of the Scriptures is a pattern of immersion that cannot be rushed or relegated to a forced march through the text under the pressure of last minute preparation. The poet-gardener engages in intentional redundancy throughout the week(s) of preaching preparation as she or he soaks in Scripture. In cognitive terms, the preacher over-learns the text until the words become second nature. In spiritual terms, the poet-gardener dwells in the Scripture until he or she can clearly hear the distinctive voice of the Author.

Attunement to the life of the community

As the strings of a guitar each have their own wave pattern but also vibrate together to produce music, the poet-gardener seeks to be in tune, attuned, to the rhythm of the Holy Spirit at work in the daily life of the community. This metaphor of attunement stands in contrast to compartmentalized ministry in which the minister operates independently and plays a series of disconnected notes throughout the week.

The poet-gardener affirms the interdependent nature of the Christian community and the organic nature of ministry. As such, she or he seeks to have a seamless ministry in which presence in the pulpit is an expression of her or his presence with the faith community in the course of daily life. For the poet-gardener, acts of ministry are more accompaniment on a journey than tasks to be performed. There is no false division between pastoral care work and the Sunday sermon. As Figure 4-1 below illustrates, the poet-gardener embraces a rhythm of attunement with the community in which preaching flows out of the experience of God's presence in all of the lived realities in which pastor and people share.

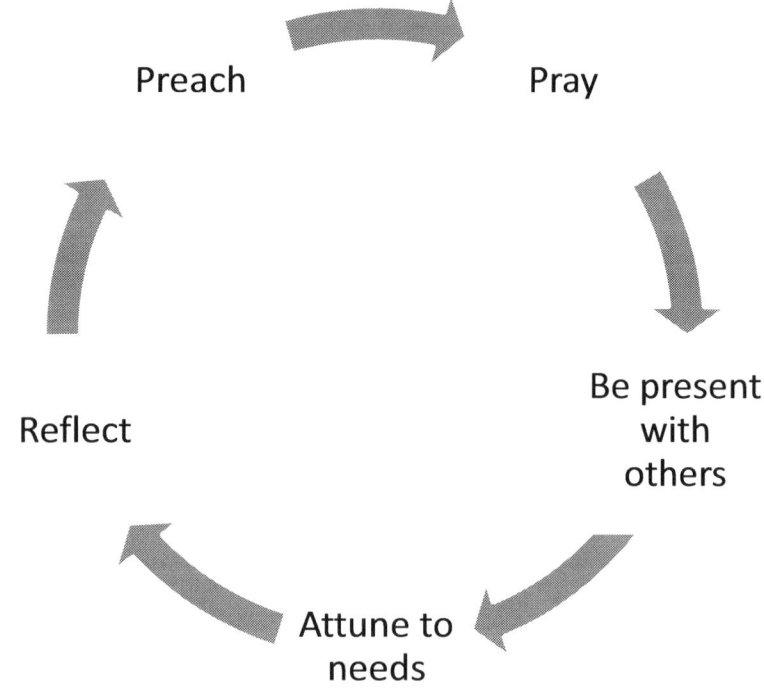

Figure 4.1: Rhythm of Attunement

Preaching in Real Time

In January 1991 the aerial bombardment of Baghdad signaled the start of the Persian Gulf War. Incredibly, millions of people around the world sat in their living rooms watching this war unfold in real time. With cameras rolling, hundreds of bombs exploded as Baghdad crumbled and history unfolded. So goes life in the twenty-first century. From reality television programs to news reports to sermons, postmodern people value communication on a metric of "reality."

To preach with presence is to preach in real time. The poet-gardener approaches preaching with attention to experiential elements that go beyond prepared speech and rhetorical persuasion. Steven Chandler suggests that the real time dimension of presence in preaching is a moment when, "The message and the messenger blend or, more accurately, fully integrate with the Spirit's ministry."[283] The preacher cooperates with the Holy Spirit in the moment through an attitude of openness to God's leading and an eagerness to keep in step with the rhythm of God's movement. These steps of integration with the work of the Spirit also involve a letting go of human agendas, a willingness to set aside prepared comments in favor of a fresh word from God.

A second "real time" quality of incarnational preaching is immediacy. In contrast to didactic approaches to sermons that utilize a third person voice and offer commentary about the Scriptures and God's activity in the world, preaching with presence is a direct, immediate encounter with God. The poet-gardener seeks to enable first person, first-order experiences about which listeners might later comment, "It was one of those God moments that I can't explain . . . You just needed to be there."

Immediacy happens when the focus is on genuine experience rather than recounting events, interpreting facts, or describing something. The poet-gardener pays sharp attention to the sensory, physical pathways of immediate experience. She or he creates sensory experiences without explaining them, allowing the community to make sense of them. Even more, the goal in preaching with presence is not only to create vivid experiences for others, but also to enjoy a vivid, fresh experience of God's Word as the core movement of preaching.

Joe Harding uses the metaphor of movie making to describe the way in which he fosters immediacy in preaching. Characterizing the movement of the sermon as a motion

---

[283] Steven Chandler, "Incarnational Ministry," *Encounter, Journal for Pentecostal Ministry,* vol.3, no. 1, Summer 2006, 1-5.

picture, Harding suggests that the preacher must first see the scenes of the movies in his or her own mind's eye before making the scenes visible to the congregation: "What I see, the congregation also sees."[284]

Being Yourself: Personhood Dynamics in Incarnational Preaching

On a human level, to preach with presence requires being yourself in the pulpit. Twenty-first century people measure a preacher's believability on the basis of authenticity and availability in the preaching moment. In other words, listeners must have a sense of who the preacher is before they will receive what she or he has to say. Commentators on the postmodern Church characterize preaching with presence as whole personality preaching.[285] Here the emphasis is on the whole-hearted investment of the preacher in the message, and more than that, in the lives of the people. The credibility of the sermon directly corresponds to the congregation's sense that the preacher is fully present and fully committed to them and the message.

Jack Roland Murphy, better known as "Murph the Surf," has preached all over the world in settings ranging from prisons to churches. His famous tag line is, "If you're not doing God's business, you're just doing time."[286] Murphy served eighteen years in prison for murder and for participating in the robbery of the American Museum of Natural History in which he stole the Star of India diamond. Despite his ignominious past, Murph the Surf is known as an inspiring preacher who communicates a challenging message of faith. When asked why they found Murphy inspiring and worth hearing, a group of men

---

[284] Joe Harding, *Have I Told You Lately?* (Nashville: Church Growth Press, 1986), 33-35.
[285] Post Modern Preaching, Incarnational Preaching," http://www.postmodernpreaching.net/incarnational.html, p. 1-3, (accessed August 14, 2008).
[286] Jack Roland Murphy, *Jewels for the Journey* (New York: International Prison Ministry, 1990), 4.

who heard him speak at a retreat in Leesburg, Florida described the experience as "Authentic-The real deal from a con man who's gone straight."[287]

This listener feedback points to the power of authenticity in the pulpit. People do not believe the preacher because they perceive him or her to be perfect. People listen to those whom they consider to be real and genuine. Authenticity involves a paradoxical mix of intentionality and self-forgetfulness. In seeking to be authentic, the poet-gardener is intentional about rigorous honesty in his or her words. Equally, authentic presence in the pulpit requires a non-defensive attitude that communicates the preacher has nothing to hide and nothing to prove.

John the Baptist summarized the self-forgetful attitude behind preaching with presence when he commented about Jesus, "He must become greater; I must become less" (John 3:30). The poet-gardener affirms that the preacher is fully present but is not the center of attention in the sermon. Rather, he or she preaches out of a transparency that reveals the preacher's genuine commitment to Christ and personal need for the redeeming work of God in the details of life.

---

[287] Interviews by author of attendees at United Methodist Men's Retreat, Leesburg, Florida, 1991.

Image Two: The Wise Fool

"If any one of you thinks he is wise by the standards of this age, he should become a fool so that he may become wise. For the wisdom of this world is foolishness in God's sight" (1 Corinthians 3:18, 19).

Mr. Bean Goes to Church

http://www.youtube.com/watch?v=-bm9mhX1q4o

"Mr. Bean Goes To Church" offers an outrageously funny satire on the joyless experience of attending church.[288] All of the elements of over-serious, institutionalized religion appear in caricature form: Unfriendly people who reluctantly share a pew, bewildering ritual, sleep inducing boredom, and incomprehensible preaching. Underlying all of Mr. Bean's experience in church is a joyless rigidity in which folks are going through the motions of a worship service that lacks any meaning to the newcomer. To make matters worse, Mr. Bean does not seem to know the implicit rules of proper church

---

[288] *Mr. Bean in Church*, directed by Rowan Atkinson and John Davies, London Atkinson, Rowan and Davies, John Howard, Polygram Video, 2003.

behavior. He plays in church-looking all around at the ornate icons and appointments, eating candy, moving in rhythm to the music.

The portrayal of preaching in this humorous vignette is particularly poignant. The viewer's experience is one-dimensional, auditory, as the preacher never appears on camera. Instead, the film focuses on Mr. Bean's experience as a listener. He hears a garbled, unintelligible message delivered in a sing-song monotone cadence. Mr. Bean finds it impossible to pay attention as he fidgets and eventually falls sound asleep. The filmmaker strongly conveys his opinion of preaching: Sermons are a boring waste of time.

To counter boredom, the tendency in preaching is to attempt to make sermons more entertaining, or at least interesting. To this end, preachers may draw upon jokes and anecdotal humor, colorful illustrations, and elements of surprise. Roger Ailes suggests that speakers, including preachers, have a narrow window of opportunity to grab the attention of listeners-about the first ninety seconds of presentation. If the speaker has not engaged listeners in this earliest stage, they likely will tune out everything else that is said.[289]

And yet, engagement and entertainment are not synonyms. Even as the preacher seeks to be deeply connected with listeners, he or she is seeking to edify, not simply titillate. In truth, engaging elements of preaching rely more upon the personhood of the preacher than rhetorical techniques. Heije Faber comments: "To represent Christ is a way of being, in the deepest sense, an attitude, that changes the climate of the

---

[289] Roger Ailes, *You Are the Message* (New York: Doubleday, 1995), 28.

congregation."²⁹⁰ The paradoxical image of the wise fool points to a way of being with the congregation which breaks through the numbness of routine speech and expected behavior to offer people a fresh glimpse of God's Word.

Childlikeness of Wise Fools

In commenting on the image of the wise fool, Alastair Campbell suggests that the wise fool is one who sets aside "adult wisdom" in favor of becoming childlike. For him, adult wisdom entails communication within the confines of social conventions that keep speech politically correct, polite, and resigned to the facts of life. In this sense, adult wisdom stands in tension with spiritual childlikeness which is characterized by innocence, naiveté, and wonder. The poet-gardener seeks to set aside the pretense of adult speech in favor of following Jesus' calling to become like a child (Matthew 18:3).²⁹¹

Campbell paints a picture of the wise fool as one known by his or her vulnerability and smallness. Like a circus clown, there is nothing overwhelming or awe inspiring. He or she engages the audience by building a kind of solidarity. When preaching out of the image of the wise fool, the preacher intimates to the congregation that he or she shares with them in boundary situations of life: sorrow, embarrassment, absurdity, setbacks. And, the audience is "with him or her" through the preacher's confident buoyancy that relies upon the strength of God, not the competence of the messenger. In this sense, the preacher's smallness allows him or her to be part of the

---

²⁹⁰Heije Faber, The Minister in the Hospital," in *Pastoral Care in the Modern Hospital,* trans. Hugo DeWaal (Philadelphia: Westminster, 1971), 92.
²⁹¹ Alastair V. Campbell, "Wise Folly," in *Rediscovering Pastoral Care* (Philadelphia: Westminster Press, 1981), 55-71.

great story of salvation without ever being the central character. As a wise fool, the greatness of the preacher is in his or her smallness.[292]

Simplicity: The Foolish but Wise Method

The image of the wise fool commends simplicity as the manner and method of preaching. Sometimes, the complex details of the preaching process become obstacles rather than tools for effective communication. Communication theorists, notably Chip and Dan Heath, have coined the term, "curse of knowledge," for the tendency in communication to make a message overly complex.[293] Preachers suffer from a forgetfulness of life on the other side of the pulpit, that is, the point of view of the uninitiated listener who does not spend his or her life immersed in theological thought. The wise fool remembers what it is like to be uninformed. True wisdom entails the ability to communicate the deep truths of God in simple, everyday categories.

Commenting on the need for simplicity, Alastair Campbell asserts: "The greatest hazard facing us in trying to help others is our verbosity. We use words to distance ourselves from experience-our own and other people's-and so lose the simple sense of nearness, of nature, of people, of God."[294] Preachers tend to have too much to say. This is Campbell's plain meaning.

An additional implication of simplicity is its power to create a sense of immediacy. Many words and complex ideas tend to distance listeners from the Gospel and an experience of God. The wise fool takes the simple approach, making no claim to special wisdom or knowledge.

---

[293]Chip Heath and Dan Heath, *Made to Stick: Why Some Ideas Survive and Others Die*, 39-40.
[294] Alastair Campbell, "Wise Folly," 55-71.

Enigmatic Loyalty: The Motivation of the Wise Fool

If simplicity is the method of the wise fool, Campbell suggests enigmatic loyalty is the motive. Christian preaching is driven by loyalties to Christ that make no sense to the world at large. Jesus repeatedly violates worldly categories of self-preservation and self-promotion as he calls his followers to a loyalty that involves loss of self. "If anyone would come after me, he must deny himself and take up his cross and follow me. For whoever wants to save his life will lose it, but whoever loses his life for me will find it" (Matthew 16:24, 25). When the preacher speaks of such loyalty to Christ, he or she is modeling a devotion that is far removed from the cultural norm. One should not assume that the listeners "get it." In fact, a call of loyalty to Christ at the expense of one's self-interest is both counter-cultural and counter-intuitive.

A word of caution is in order. If the preacher does not genuinely hold enigmatic loyalty to Christ, he or she should not make a false claim of dying devotion. The congregation has a "sniff sense" for falsehood where the preacher's motives are concerned. Even if they are not listening, they are watching for evidence of true motives.

In a sense, people are inextricably drawn to the preacher who claims such a nonsensical loyalty to Christ. Curiosity gets the better of them. Why would anyone deny himself or herself for Christ, giving up the sure things of worldly success for a handful of promises in the Bible? And yet, researchers of every ilk agree that humans have this same longing for a greater than, a higher loyalty in life than one's own selfish interests.[295] Here is the paradox of the preacher who is the wise fool. At the same time she or he

---

[295] For a review of theological and secular literature on spirituality and meaning making, see Kenneth J. Collins, *Exploring Christian Spirituality: An Ecumenical Reader* (Grand Rapids, MI: Baker Academic, 2000).

expresses a loyalty to Christ as a central core value, the preacher risks everything in pursuit of that loyalty.

Prophetic Voice of the Wise Fool

The third quality of the wise fool is the voice in which he or she speaks: the prophet. The image here is not a booming, over powering voice but one of subtlety and surprise. In reflecting on the prophetic voice of fools, Heije Faber observes: "It is no accident that in the courts of the mighty the jester alone had the freedom to say what he liked."[296] The wise fool specializes in utilizing misdirection and self-effacement to reveal what has been overlooked or dismissed Operating as a wise fool, the preacher utilizes ironic insight as a necessary corrective to arrogance and pomposity.

What mode of prophetic proclamation might the wise fool image promote? Laughter lies at the core. When one laughs, he or she expresses freedom in the midst of life's exigencies. Laughter recognizes the absurdity of worldly claims of certainty and control. To laugh in the face of over-serious circumstances is to challenge the norms and authorities of the world.

Citing the medieval practice of the Narranfest or Feast of Fools, Campbell points to ways that laughter confronts institutional self-importance. From the first of January until the Feast of the Epiphany, young clergy would put on a parody of church practices, a sort of anti-Mass, complete with a lord donkey, to mock the liturgical rigidity of the church. Although celebration of the Feast of Fools was repeatedly banned, generations of young clergy continued to practice the farcical observance. The church wrote off Narranfest as a rebellious expression of youthful foolishness. And yet, the Feast of Fools

---

300 Heije Faber, The Minister in the Hospital," 84.

offered the church a sort of prophetic mirror to see her excesses and self-absorbed institutional life.[297]

Donald Capps emphasizes the power of the wise fool to reframe life situations. He suggests that the simplicity of the wise fool reframes the oppressive quality of overwhelming problems by offering an ironic discernment of "something to smile about" even in the darkest hour. In simple ways, folly discerns that part of the problem has to do with the anxious tendency to make problems worse than they are, layering complexity upon complexity. Ironically, the fool seems to be missing the complex details of problems at the same time he or she is cutting to the chase. Simplicity reframes by discerning that problems are simpler than they appear.

In exercising enigmatic loyalty, the wise fool comes against the notion that anyone is a hopeless case. In unswerving loyalty to Christ and faith in his redemptive power, the preacher refuses to believe that anyone can sink below the power of Christ to save. The wise fool reframes the natural tendency to "cut our losses" into a renewed faith that all things are possible with God.

Finally, Capps suggests that laughter itself is a reframing act. It has a releasing power that is a physical expression of freedom. The common aphorism, "Sometimes, you just have to laugh," may be a profound statement of faith. Here one admits that we live in an ironic world where God acts paradoxically. To claim faith in God with full acceptance of God's paradoxical ways is to reframe the human demand that God give a sign of God's reality and compassion.[298]

---

[297] Alastair Campbell, "Wise Folly," 55-71.
[298] Donald Capps, "The Wise Fool Reframes," in *Reframing: A New Method in Pastoral Care* (Minneapolis: Fortress Press, 1990), 1-8 and 169-182.
[298] Heije Faber, The Minister in the Hospital," 84.

Clowning for Christ

In a closely related metaphor, Heije Faber offers the circus clown as an image for ministry. This is an especially useful metaphor for reflecting on the role of the preacher in the faith community. Faber comments about the importance of the clown in making sense of life: "The clown has his own place in our world, much more than a joker or funny guy. He brings home to us an aspect of life that we need to make the world tolerable."[299] The clown offers a different perspective. As the audience holds its collective breath in terror while a performer sticks his head inside a tiger's mouth, the clown reminds them that it is only an illusion; they are safe in their seats. In other words, the clown helps people reclaim the perspective of reality.

Faber suggests that the life of a clown is filled with tensions that parallel the role of a preacher. The clown is part of the circus troupe, but he or she operates in isolation. While trapeze artists are the main attraction, clowns are off in a side-ring offering the relief of comic distraction. The clown operates out of a posture of absurd disconnection. He or she is slightly anti-social, always on the fringes with a kind of carefreeness and inner freedom.

Equally, the clown is an amateur among experts. He offers little to "wow" the crowd:

"He reveals his small, powerless self while operating out of a sense of innocence and naiveté; the clown relates as a child-like person. In those little, funny people he plays the part with a smile, playing like children amongst big guns, allowing what is threatening to be seen for what it is: powerless and ridiculous."[300]

---

303 Heije Faber, The Minister in the Hospital," 84.
304 Ibid.

The image of the clown also points to the tension between studied preparation and creative spontaneity in the act of preaching. A clown act that is too precise and predictable comes across as contrived-unbelievable and boring. So too, over-reliance on preparation produces sermons that are wooden and difficult to hear. And yet, professional clowns are quite expert in their high jinks. Their silly falls and pranks appear spontaneous because they have become an effortless part of the clown persona through hours of careful practice.

In the same way, the preacher must learn and carefully practice the craft of preaching so that it becomes second nature, lacking self-consciousness. In the image of the clown, the preacher becomes willing for others to laugh at him or her when operating out of an inner assurance of God-given competence. Even more, the preacher is prepared to laugh with the people, unafraid of perceptions of incompetence, incompleteness, or frailty. The laughter of preaching is evidence of an inner freedom that validates the presence of God among God's people. One might say that the ultimate "craft" of preaching is a joyous, intentional openness to the Holy Spirit.

Image Three: The Gardener

"I planted the seed, Apollos watered it, but God made it grow. So neither he who plants nor he who waters is anything, but only God, who makes things grow. The man who plants and the man who waters have one purpose and each will be rewarded according to his own labor. For we are God's fellow laborers" (1 Corinthians 3:6-9).

As Good As It Gets

http://www.youtube.com/watch?v=FbyP8gbb1hw

"You make me want to be a better man."[301] This line from the film, *As Good As It Gets,* epitomizes the kind of impact that the poet-gardener seeks to have on people. The preacher is motivated by the hope that the seeds of God's Word sown week in and week out might produce fruit of a new "want power," new priorities in life. Like a gardener, he or she tends the plants and tills the soil in faith that the fruit will come in God's timing.

God at Work in the Ordinary

As Good As It Gets offers a number of parallels to the work of the gardener that might inform preaching. Jack Nicholson portrays the central character, Melvin Udall, a

---

[301] *As Good As It Gets,* directed by Mark Andrus and James L. Brooks, Tri-Star Pictures, 1997.

man trapped in an ironic life. Melvin is a successful romance novel writer considered to be an expert in relationships by millions of devoted readers. And yet, he cannot practice what he preaches. Melvin suffers from obsessive-compulsive disorder to the extent that he is hyper-isolated, eschewing contact with all but a handful of people. One of the few people whom Melvin permits daily contact is Carol (played by Helen Hunt), a waitress at the diner where Melvin eats all of his meals. She has become an unwitting part of his obsessive-compulsive rituals. Melvin will only eat meals served by Carol at his designated table.

From these narrow circumstances, Carol eventually becomes a person with life changing influence in Melvin's life. Without even trying, she motivates Melvin to look at his life in a different way. Ironically, Carol is simply attending to the details of waiting on customers. And yet, by being the wholesome person she is, she ignites a love within Melvin that shakes him to the core. In his own words, she makes him want to be a better man.

Carol is an ordinary person. The influence she exerts on others arises more out of her self-acceptance of who she is than any attempt to be extraordinary. She does not have any clinical, specialized insight into Melvin's problems. At more than one point in the story, Carol expresses her dismay at his neurotic, self-centered attitudes, admitting that his problems far exceed her know-how. And yet, she becomes a powerful change agent for Melvin. She is a living parable of Carl Rogers' model of personal efficacy: "If we are truly ourselves, we have enough. As you become more whole yourself, you are able to use all of your experience. You discover that you have within you what you need."[302]

---

[302]Carl Rogers in *Cultivating Wholeness: A Guide to Care and Counseling in Faith Communities.*, 54.

The preacher can take heart in the many ironic parallels of preaching with this story line. So often, he or she faces listeners who seem to be a waste of time. Many persons in the congregation appear to be marginally committed, inattentive, and in attendance for wrong reasons. Like Melvin, they are anxious, isolated persons, faces in the crowd who wish to remain anonymous. The preacher is acutely aware that his or her relationship to these listeners is tenuous. He or she cannot force any agenda with such persons and is helpless to control their choices or behavior.

And yet, the preacher is far from powerless. Like a gardener laboring in obscurity, the work he or she is doing is crucially important work for plants that do not-cannot- acknowledge or affirm the gardener. Here is the import of Paul's comment in 1 Corinthians 3:6-9: The gardener is never the central player, just the instrument of God's plan for fruitfulness in human life. God is the one who does the growing.

The preacher is an ordinary person like Carol the waitress. By just being herself, she offers Melvin a role model of a healthy person who has character qualities he wishes to have in his own life. The healing power of this casual relationship stands in sharp contrast to the impotence of the clinical relationship Melvin has with his psychiatrist. Melvin has spent thousands of dollars and hundreds of hours attending weekly psychiatric treatments that provide little relief from his neuroses. In despair he comments to another patient in the waiting room, "What if this is as good as it gets?"[303]

Few would guess a waitress would be more helpful than a psychiatrist in helping one with mental health problems. Modern culture inculcates the notion that specialization and professionalism are the answers to our most complicated problems. Preachers, too,

---

[303] *As Good As It Gets,* Tri-Star Pictures, 1997.

are tempted to take on a professional image as those whose sermons work with surgical precision in addressing people's problems.

Obsession with professionalism stands in sharp contrast to the gardener image. As a gardener, the preacher employs a simple approach to change and growth. The gardener is attentive to the details of the ground and the plants. The garden sets the agenda. That is to say, effective gardeners do not enter the garden with an inflexible "to do" list for the day. Instead, he or she spends time observing and enjoying the garden, taking note of new growth, looking for tell-tale signs of disease or problems. The gardener works, providing services for the garden that are needed at the moment. This regular attention to small details is essential to the garden's survival. There is an intimate quality to gardening. To know how to garden, one must know the garden.

One might say that the power of the gardener lies in the mundane. The gardener's work is indirect and difficult to measure in outcomes. Attention to small details on a daily basis makes for a beautiful garden. Soil must be hoed, weeds pulled, plants watered. None of these tasks is glamorous, but they are all essential. In like manner, the preacher works as a gardener in relative obscurity. Each sermon preached attends to the needs of the community at that point in time without claiming to solve all problems for all time.

Community Care Dynamics

In exploring aspects of the gardener image, Margaret Kornfeld emphasizes the dynamism of faith communities.[304] Each time one stands to preach, the needs and strengths of the congregation are different from the time before. The preacher must work to create balance in ever-shifting communities that defy attempts at once-for-all solutions.

---

[304] Margaret Kornfeld, *Cultivating Wholeness: A Guide to Care and Counseling in Faith Communities*, 17-24.

Of course, the natural temptation is to want to control, to manage change within the congregation. More often than not, the preacher is confronted by his or her own inability to control even small details of people and congregational life.

Objectivity is a basic tenet of the scientific approach that has become a presupposition of leadership in modern thinking. The preacher, too, is tempted to unreflectively seek to render "objective" sermons that stand back from the problems and people in order to permit unemotional judgment to work.

By contrast, Kornfeld underlines the subjective nature of ministry, including preaching. As a member of the faith community, one does not preach as a detached person dispensing wisdom with no stake in the outcome. Rather, sermons articulate dimensions and details of a shared life. Claims of objectivity in preaching are facetious on two counts. First, sermons are interactive communication, an exchange of views on matters of faith. Obviously, the preacher is doing most of the talking. But, she or he is not the only one communicating.

Second, people strenuously resist and resent sermons that claim to offer an objective word about their painful, subjective lives. Unless the preacher is willing to be a subject in the community, to enter into the pain and joy of the people, sermons will fall in all likelihood on deaf ears. Sermons that stand back run the risk of eliciting a "laboratory rat" response in which listeners feel discounted and objectified by an uncaring preacher.

Since the preacher is a participant in the congregation who shares common ground with them, she or he cannot dispense sermons from a hierarchical distance. Rather, the gardener ministers in interaction with the community. More often than not, interaction begins at ugly starting points or venues. After Carol is forced to take a leave of absence from her waitress job to care for her ailing son, Melvin responds with surprising compassion. He gets involved in her life, even underwriting medical care for her ailing child. But, Melvin's true motives for these acts of kindness quickly come to the surface. He is driven more by his selfish compulsions than a desire to be helpful. Melvin needs Carol to go back to work at the diner so that he might eat.

This story drips with irony. Melvin's overwhelming life problems, his obsessions and compulsions, becomes a source of life for Carol's son. One is both repulsed by Melvin's self-absorbed attitudes and surprised by the good that can come out of the worst of human attributes. Here is a reminder that the stinking manure of human experience can become fertilizer, a source of growth in the right soil and under the right circumstances.

Like a gardener, the preacher must be willing to work with the fertilizer in the lives of others. Such preaching requires getting one's hands dirty for the sake of enriching the garden. It is a necessary part of the job. Without regular fertilizing, soil becomes anemic and fruit becomes scarce.

Here is a word of hope for those who preach in the midst of seemingly endless human problems and suffering. This "manure of life" is an important ingredient, a catalyst, to spiritual growth, not an obstacle. The response of the gardener in the face of sin and suffering is not to avoid, deny, or blame, but rather to help the congregation to engage together in working the fertilizer into the soil.

Kornfeld suggests that the gardener operates with twin attitudes that work in tension with one another. On the one hand, gardeners expect growth and change. No one invests hundreds of hours of time in a garden with the expectation that all of the plants will die. Rather, one endures the heat and boring routine of gardening with the confident expectation that it will produce flowers. On the other hand, the gardener does not know exactly when the flowers will begin to appear or how many blossoms the plants might bear. One always gardens in "docta ignota," the way of not knowing.[305]

Jesus articulates the plight of the gardener in the parable of the growing seed. "Night and day, whether he sleeps or gets up, the seed sprouts and grows, though he does not know how. All by itself, the soil produces grain" (Mark 4: 27, 28). Like a gardener, the preacher plants and tills seeds without knowing the precise impact he or she is having. For the plants to grow, it is not necessary that the gardener comprehend or be in control of every detail. To the contrary, Jesus asserts that the way of God's Kingdom is a way of not controlling, a way of not knowing. Nonetheless, the Kingdom of God is full of expectation. Plants grow in a predictable, God-ordained cycle-"first the stalk, then the head, then the full kernel in the head" (Matthew 4:28). And, the point of life is fruitfulness; there is expectation of a harvest.

One might say that the gardener is more a servant to the garden than its master. And yet, there is great power in servanthood. As the gardener creates and maintains a hospitable environment, plants thrive. In other words, the health of the garden depends upon the practice of certain forms of hospitality within the garden. In the same vein, hospitality offers far ranging possibilities for preaching. Sermons can produce spiritual fruitfulness by engineering a hospitable climate in which change can happen and people can grow.

Hospitality and Climates of Growth

---

[305] Margaret Kornfeld, *Cultivating Wholeness: A Guide to Care and Counseling in Faith Communities*, 17-24.

In *As Good As It Gets,* Carol provides one of the rare hospitable spaces in Melvin's life. He does not feel safe to eat without fear of infection in anyone else's company. Outside of his familiar table at the diner, Melvin's life is captive to the hostility and fear he feels toward all those around him. Radical isolation is an invisible prison for him as he rejects any attempts by others to make contact with him. When his neighbor, Simon, attempts to befriend him, Melvin cynically comments, "Are we done being neighbors now?"[306]

Hospitality plays a surprising sub-plot in Melvin's life story when he becomes the temporary custodian for Verdell. Verdell is a dog that has become homeless when his owner, Simon, is hospitalized with injuries from a brutal home invasion. Melvin hates dogs. To him, they are walking germ farms. A week earlier, he shoved Verdell down the garbage chute to silence his barking. Under threat from Simon's imposing friend, Melvin takes Verdell into his home. He faces the challenge to convert hostility into hospitality.

A hilarious and touching scenario ensues. Melvin and Verdell become best friends. In ways Melvin did not anticipate, Verdell brings gifts of companionship and humor into his life. Through his emerging friendship with a dog, Melvin begins to open his life to others around him. An authentic transformation from hostility to hospitality takes place when Melvin welcomes Verdell's owner, Simon, into his home while Simon convalesces from his injuries.

How might the preacher apply principles of hospitality? Contrary to popular notions of hospitality as refreshments or physical accommodations, Henri Nouwen suggests that hospitality begins with a welcoming attitude. Drawing upon the story of Abraham's visitation from the three angels (Genesis 18:1-15), he envisions hospitality as

---

[306] *As Good As It Gets,* Tri-Star Pictures, 1997.

welcoming strangers who are bearing gifts.[307] An inward shift of attitude from suspicion and fear precedes the outward invitation to dinner. In Nouwen's words, hospitality converts the "fearful stranger into the welcome guest."[308]

Hospitality is also a shift in one's expectations toward others. In hostility the human tendency is to view the stranger as threatening, an unknown person with unknown motives. In hostility, one expects strangers to cause harm. Hospitality leads one to see strangers as members of the family of God with unrealized potential for good in our lives. Our estrangement is not their fault, nor is it the final reality. In hospitality, one practices openness. The expectation is that this stranger will become a new friend who will enrich one's life.

In keeping with Nouwen's insight that hospitality is an attitude or posture of welcome, the preacher crafts sermons with word choice, body language, and tone that express, "Welcome home." In many ways, the non-anxious presence of the preacher is the welcome mat. A key part of sermon preparation and delivery is attention to one's personal level of anxiety that might be transmitted to wary listeners as "stay away."

One key factor in creating a welcoming posture is to become self-aware and intentional about one's control needs. Too often, sermons become a venue for the preacher to exert control over the thoughts and lives of others. Like the gardener who tills the garden without controlling the produce, hospitable preachers relinquish control to God and focus on creating a climate in which growth can happen. A growth climate requires nurturing elements such as acceptance, safety, and freedom to disagree.[309]

---

[307] Henri Nouwen, *Reaching Out: The Three Movements of the Spiritual Life,* 51-67.
[308] Ibid., 53.
[309] Ibid.

Equally, hospitable environments must be guarded and protected. The preacher must guard against preoccupation with being right or other ulterior motives that silently control the agenda of the sermon. He or she must remain aware of secular assumptions of comparison and competition that taint the hospitable message.

To be truly hospitable, the preacher must return to the garden, that is, affirm his or her own embeddedness in the community of faith. Yes, the preacher lovingly tends the soil and the plants. Even so, he or she is also growing in the garden, nurtured in the same soil. Hospitable preaching is a community enterprise, a partnership. The preacher sees sermons as the practice of mutual edification in which the entire community engages in revealing God's Word and reframing life in terms of what God, the Master Gardener, might yet do in our lives.

Image Four: The Poet

"For we are God's workmanship *(poiema)*, created in Christ Jesus to do good works which God prepared in advance for us to do" (Ephesians 2:10).

"I Have A Dream"

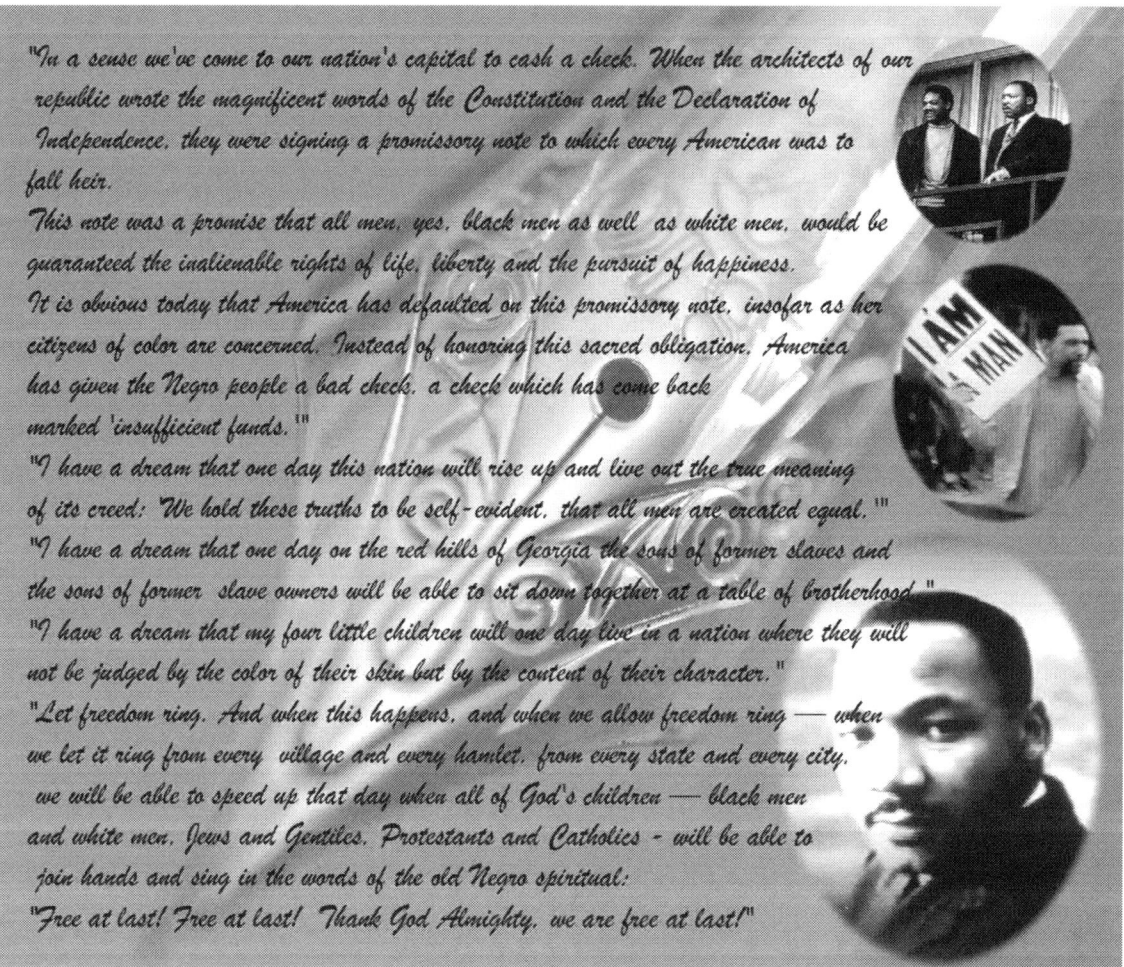

"I Have A Dream," Dr. Martin Luther King King, Jr.

"I have a dream." With these four words spoken on August 28, 1963 at the Washington Mall, Dr. Martin Luther King, Jr. set aflame the smoldering civil rights movement.[310] This image, a dream of equal opportunity for all Americans regardless of race or ethnicity, motivated thousands of persons to risk life and limb to challenge wrongful laws in a racist society. The election of Barak Obama as the first African-American U.S. president is the strongest evidence yet of the motivating power of Dr. King's poetic image, the dream. In significant measure, his dream of equality has become a reality.

Dr. King is rightly honored as an American hero and social activist, but one should not lose sight of the fact that he was a theologian and preacher first. "I Have A Dream" was more a sermon than a speech. Even more, it was poetic speech that expressed larger than life truths in ways that even the most resistant listeners could not escape hearing.

The consensus of church and society is that King spoke as a prophet. A more thoughtful examination of his sermons suggests that he preached like a poet. Ironically, King preached poetically out of a prosaic, rhetorical model of sermon design. In describing his rationale for building a sermon, King details a model that follows traditional homiletical practice: "A good, solid sermon has to have three elements which I call 'three p's': it proves an appeal to the intellect, it paints an appeal for the imagination, and it persuades an appeal for the heart."[311]

---

[310] Martin Luther King, Jr., "The I have a dream speech," http://www.usconstitution.net/dream, (accessed July 20, 2009).

[311] Mervyn A. Warren, *King Came Preaching: The Pulpit Power of Dr. Martin Luther King, Jr.* (Downers Grove, Illinois: InterVarsity Press, 2001), 90-91.

How might one describe poetic preaching? Clearly, this image refers to more than including some poetry in the sermon for illustrative purposes. The poet draws upon three dynamics in sermons. He or she preaches poetic justice beyond human laws and sense of fairness. The poet preaches with poetic license, a sense of freedom that comes through living under the authority of God. And, the preacher is God's *poiema,* an expression of God's creative work in his or her personhood.

Poetic Justice

"The most popular preachers are those who can preach soothing sermons on 'How to be happy' and 'How to relax.' Some have been tempted to re-translate Jesus' command to read, 'Go ye into all the world and keep your blood pressure down and lo I will make you a well-adjusted personality.' All of this is indicative of the fact that it is midnight in the inner lives of men and women."[312]

Walter Brueggemann points to poetic justice at work when he characterizes preaching as "A poetic construal of an alternative world . . .an act of relentless hope."[313] In this comment he goes beyond communication categories for poetic preaching to speak of the theological implications. Brueggemann suggests that sermons work for poetic justice in a climate in which the gospel is "A truth widely held, but a truth greatly reduced . . .The gospel is simply an old habit among us."[314] Poetic justice comes as preaching that casts alternative visions for understanding reality. Here the preacher challenges his or her listeners' assumptions about the way things are. The poetic preacher suggests that the "settled facts" are open to dialogue. More than that, transformation is at work through the gift of God's grace doing something new.

For more than twenty-five years, Walter Cronkite, CBS news anchor, concluded his telecast by saying, "That's the way it is." Cronkite's signature sign-off summarizes

---

[312] Martin Luther King, Jr. "A Knock at Midnight," in *King Came Preaching,* 93.
[313] Walter Brueggemann, *Finally Comes the Poet: Daring Speech for Proclamation,* 6.
[314] Ibid. 1.

the prosaic worldview. Prosaic sermons run the risk of preaching, "That's the way it is," instead of the evangelical truth, "Forget the former things; do not dwell on the past. Behold, I am doing a new thing!" (Isaiah 43:18, 19). Brueggemann bemoans the ways in which the counter-cultural truth of Scripture has been co-opted in preaching. Instead of unleashing the irresistible force of God's Kingdom, sermons often reduce the Scripture to an ingredient in a status quo, prosaic worldview. Too often, preachers are tempted to use the pulpit as an advice column, offering diminutive messages on how to muddle through life as it is in a more spiritual way. Brueggemann suggests that poetic preachers must engage in "counter speak" that restores the more than, bigger than expected voice of the Scriptures. He comments, "Reduced speech leads to reduced lives. Sunday morning is the practice of a counter life through counter speech. To address the issues of a truth greatly reduced requires us to be poets that speak against a prose world."[315]

Of all the obstacles to poetic justice faced by the preacher, over-confident certitude may represent the highest and broadest. When people are certain they are right, and that God certifies their rightness, little change is possible. Brueggemann suggests that the constant tendency in the church is toward confident certitude, the conclusion that we understand God's Word, have interpreted it correctly, and are applying it faithfully to our lives.[316]

In a paradoxical way, prophetic justice works to create doubt. Of course, the preacher does not suggest that one doubt God or God's promises. But the poetic preacher does seek to remind the people of the edginess of God's Word, a word humans do not

---

[315] Walter Brueggemann, *Finally Comes the Poet: Daring Speech for Proclamation*, 3.
[316] Ibid.

control and manage. He or she seeks to cast doubt on the smugness and possessiveness of our faith.

Herein lies the brilliance of King's "I Have A Dream" sermon. He was able to communicate faith in a secular environment; he engendered hope in an environment of despair. King preached poetic justice for people of color in a historical context in which the majority in power already had its mind made up on the subject. His sermon, "I Have a Dream," challenged these misguided assumptions poetically through the compelling image of the "bounced check, marked insufficient funds." And yet, King's sermon did not degenerate into a bitter diatribe. At the same time he convicted mainstream America of injustice toward marginalized persons, he also invited all to take part in the dream. "I have a dream" not only challenged wrong assumptions; it offered an alternative vision. King uncorked the motivating power of prophetic justice.

Mervyn Warren suggests that Dr. King's sermons operated out of a "constructive conceptualization." By this term Warren refers to a marriage of analytical and imaginative capacities that worked together to build new meaning.[317] King exhibited extraordinary powers of reason in his persuasive sermons. However, his arguments for justice would likely have fallen on deaf ears had they been reduced to another set of essays against American apartheid. Martin Luther King's genius was his ability to seek poetic justice.

Poetic License

At a basic level, poetic license has to do with the way the preacher uses words. Of course, words are the building blocks of meaning in prose as well as poems. And yet, the

---

[317] Mervyn Warren, *King Came Preaching: The Pulpit Power of Dr. Martin Luther King, Jr.*, 76-77.

common ingredient of words does not suggest that prose and poetry are basically the same thing.

Sand is the principal ingredient in both a beach and in blown glass. Nonetheless, one would never confuse a beach with a glass bowl. To convert a beach into beautiful hand-blown glass requires fire, skill, and courage. Likewise, poetic preaching flows molten out of the heart and mind of the preacher with a burning in his bones. In poetic preaching a conversion of words takes place. The prosaic, assumptive use of words is transformed into something qualitatively different. Human words become a divine Word through the conveyance of prophetic imagination. Poetic preachers like Martin Luther King, Jr. are preachers whose sermons are forged in the fire of the Holy Spirit (Matthew 3:11).

Poetic license is the overflow of an inner freedom that permits the poet to offer alternative meanings for words and alternative views of the world. As a figure of speech, "poetic license" refers to the freedom one exercises in handling facts in an imaginative and unexpected way for the sake of creating an artistic impression. In the case of the poetic preacher, authorization for poetic license comes from God who called him or her to preach. Brueggemann suggests that poetic preaching is actually "another language," a God-given language, in which the real goes beyond our narrow understanding of the facts. To exercise poetic license is to speak paradoxically. Poetic speech involves a subtlety that confronts without affronting, a forcefulness that is not domineering, a reality that includes imaginative possibilities.[318]

Martin Luther King, Jr. employed a form of poetic narrative which embodied these elements of license. This is not to suggest that King used a lot of story illustrations

---

[318]Walter Brueggemann, *Finally Comes the Poet: Daring Speech for Proclamation*, 141.

in his sermons; he did not. Rather, he understood that the dominant narrative of American history perpetuated the image of black people as slaves despite the Emancipation Proclamation. The historical assignation, "slaves," condemned people of color to second-class citizenship and gave white Americans permission to enact laws that perpetuated a caste system. For lasting change to happen, America needed a more accurate and redemptive understanding of its narrative history. When King quotes a line from a patriotic song, "Let freedom ring," he reframes its historic meaning. Now, freedom's ringing bell is sounding for all Americans, not certain classes or races.[319]

Poetic narrative is the language of prophetic imagination. Walter Brueggemann suggests that prophetic imagination begins in remembering God's faithful character and promises. To remember what God had to say permits one to recover the truth, untainted by the prejudicial interpretations of the dominant culture.[320]

In retelling the story with different assumptions and interpretations, poetic narrative confronts the "normal" way of telling the community's story that has been labeled as history. Poetic preachers like Martin Luther King, Jr. acknowledge that history is largely a history of power, the power of one group of people over another. In recounting a sacred history, poetic narrative takes the license to attribute power in history to God. Acknowledging God's sovereignty in history calls into question the sovereignty by violent force of one people over another.

Here is the source of freedom from enslavement to societal standards such as caste systems and apartheid. When King says, "I have a dream," he is pointing to the poetic possibility of alternative paths that arise out of this confrontation with historical

---

[319] Martin Luther King, Jr., "The I Have A Dream Speech."
[325] Walter Brueggemann, *The Prophetic Imagination*, 38-41.

enslavement. His poetic narrative empowered his listeners to draw new conclusions from the story line and to believe that alternative futures might be in reach.

In confronting the assumptive world of Americans, King ran the risk of being misinterpreted. Indeed, he was labeled a Communist and subjected to criminal investigation by the Federal Bureau of Investigation. When the message is unwelcome, poetic license may be readily dismissed as fantasy or outright falsehood. Brueggemann suggests that preachers employ poetic license to offer fiction, not to be confused with falsehood or fantasy. The term "fiction" suggests an alternative reality that cannot be managed, vetted, and reduced to data points. He equates fiction with the Kingdom of God where the story is not yet finished; the conclusion is certain but beyond the horizon.[321]

When King preached, "I have a dream," he engaged a metaphor that represented the paradox of poetic license. Dreams, in and of themselves, are paradoxical experiences. One's dreams can be vivid while defying description. A dream can be compelling, even life changing, but others cannot see it. King's goal in "I have a dream" was not to offer an informative talk on the phenomenon of dreams, but rather to inculcate a dream of God's alternative future in the hearts of his listeners. To accomplish this goal required a poetic reframing. King offers a number of poetic snapshots of his dream that move from a very personal dream of opportunity for his own children, to a dream of other children holding hands in friendship, to a dream of equality and freedom for all people.

Poiema: Personhood of the Poet

In commenting on Dr. King's preaching ethos, Mervyn Warren focuses on King's personhood as both the expression and validation of his ethos. On the subject of personhood in the pulpit, Dr. King himself commented: "One must not only preach a

---

[321] Walter Brueggemann, *The Prophetic Imagination*, 38-41.

sermon with his voice, he must preach it with his life."[322] In other words, the message and the messenger are inseparable where the poet preacher is concerned.

In Warren's analysis, an important dynamic of King's personhood was empathy. He suggests that King's heartfelt empathy for the suffering of black people in America gave an energizing quality to his sermons. King preached with tears in his eyes. He did not stop at offering commentary on the suffering of black people in America; he shared the suffering. Over a decade, he endured repeated jailing (more than twenty times), threats, the bombing of his home, and eventually, assassination. Even as King shared the suffering of his people, he also shared an empathic hope. His dream of a different, more just world included not only others' children, but his own children. "I have a dream that my four little children will one day live in a nation where they will not be judged by the color of their skin but by the content of their character. I have a dream today."[323]

A second aspect of Martin Luther King's personhood was his uncommon competence as a preacher. The public, even his enemies, bought into King's image as a competent minister based on his advanced education and impressive credentials. Beyond the image of competence, he possessed the substance. He demonstrated an inspiring degree of balance and unflappability. And yet, he was thoroughly grounded. King preached with a buoyant hopefulness; he operated without illusion as to the steady dangers he faced in his work. "Do not despair if you are condemned and persecuted for righteousness' sake. When you testify for truth and justice, you are liable to scorn."[324]

King's personal competence showed up as well in his lack of defensiveness and arrogance. When attacked by others, he responded in keeping with his message of non-violence. When physically attacked on stage by a white youth at a meeting of the

---

[322] Mervyn Warren, *King Came Preaching*, 78.
[323] Martin Luther King, Jr., "The I Have A Dream Speech."
[324] Martin Luther King, Jr., "Paul's Letter to American Christians) in *King Came Preaching*, 78.

Southern Christian Leadership Conference, King refused to file charges against the young man. Such a response displayed not only self-control but also wisdom of example. King could hardly call people to eschew a violent response in the face of attack dogs and high-pressure hoses if he was unwillingly to model this radical approach.

Martin Luther King's sense of personal dignity was a particularly prophetic quality of his personhood. Although he was a relatively small man in physical stature, his personal bearing and posture-head high, chest out-conveyed confidence and strength. His words confirmed deep convictions about human dignity. "I have a dream that one day this nation will rise up and live out the true meaning of its creed: 'We hold these truths to be self-evident: that all men are created equal.' We must forever conduct our struggle on the high plane of dignity and discipline."[325] King's dignity was a living defiance to Jim Crow laws that treated black people as second-class citizens. And, his accomplishments as a person served as an inspiring example to down-trodden persons who lacked hope of ever being different.

---

[325] Martin Luther King, Jr., "The I Have A Dream Speech."

EPILOGUE

So What?

Dr. Fred Craddock, my mentor and seminary professor in preaching, taught me to write this two-word question, "So, What?" at the top of my sermon notes. It is an appropriate question of this book as well. Publishing research data indicate that 2,501 books and other media on the subject of preaching were published during the five-year period, 2004-2009.[326] Ironically, not a single title among these works included the phrases, "poet-gardener" or "soul care preaching." What might these publishing statistics mean? At the very least, the absence of research and writing on the relationship between soul care and preaching suggests that this has been a neglected angle of vision on preaching.

In a sense, *Poet-Gardener* asks, "So what?" in order to start a new conversation around a very old subject: preaching. This is a conversation of vital importance to the Church and the world. Paul wrote to the church at Rome to respond to the "So what?" questions of his time:

"How, then, can they call on the One they have not believed in? And how can they believe in the One of whom they have not heard? And how can they hear without someone preaching to them? And how can they preach unless they are sent?" (Romans 10:14, 15).

The Scriptures are no less true for the twenty-first century than they were for the first century. Despite the fact that preaching has been marginalized by the Church in many venues and has endured a bad reputation in common parlance, a strange fact remains. Preaching is still God's chosen, foolish way to communicate God's

---

[326] Statistics provided by Jill Branscum, research librarian, Anderson University Nicholson Library, August 1, 2009. For further details, WorldCat search engine provides data on publishing by subject.

transforming love and truth. What then are the implications of the poet-gardener model of soul care preaching for the future?

Implications for Further Research

As a theological educator, my mind goes immediately to this question: What does *Poet-Gardener* imply for the way that seminaries train preachers? With rare exception, homiletical training in seminaries focuses sharply on the technicalities of sermon preparation and delivery. This is not a bad or unnecessary focus. However, *Poet-Gardener* challenges those who teach preachers to attend to dimensions of preaching that have been largely neglected.

A first area for additional research in homiletical pedagogy centers on the need for a more integrated approach. By necessity pastoral training requires that students take classes in diverse subjects related to ministry. The upside of traditional seminary classes is depth of study in various disciplines. The downside is that newly minted ministers often emerge from seminary without an integrated view of ministry. And, the pulpit is the weekly venue where congregational ministers must publicly integrate their faith. If the preacher fails to connect the dots between preaching, pastoral care, and spiritual formation of the congregation, his or her pulpit ministry will be marginalized to a weekly worship ritual perceived to be largely irrelevant to the life challenges of people.

Poet-Gardener challenges theological educators to consider ways that preaching might be integrated into Biblical studies, pastoral care, and constructive theology courses. In doing so, the seminary is singing the song of the local church. The standard question of ministry candidates is: "Can he or she preach?" The answer lies in the ability of the minister to integrate and interpret the many dimensions of pastoral ministry into a comprehensible, engaging sermon that cares for the souls of people.

When I came as a faculty candidate to the seminary where I teach, a search committee member asked me: "Do you teach a subject or do you teach people?" Of course, the best answer is "Yes." Integrated training in homiletics requires that the educational process engage persons and content. The challenge is to hold together formation of the personhood of the preacher with the training of the mind. Put more simply, one might say that integrated training addresses both the head and heart of the student.

Poet-Gardener underlines the importance of the personhood of the preacher. As such, the model commends a second area of additional research: personhood development. If the preacher is not a person of faith or is not believable, his or her message will return empty. How can seminaries do a more effective job in helping ministerial candidates to engage in a lifelong journey of conformation to the character of Christ, the paragon of healthy personhood?

Raising questions about personhood development is an important beginning. Traditionally, seminaries have listed toward a "think tank" approach which deals almost exclusively with intellectual and academic development. This traditional model operates with standard academic courses not unlike any other graduate school. However, recent research such as the work of Charles Foster et al, suggests that effectiveness in ministry, including preaching, flows out of a cocktail of intellectual acuity, emotional intelligence, personal competence, and spiritual vitality.[327]

---

[327] Charles R. Foster, et al., *Educating Clergy: Teaching Practices and Pastoral Imagination* (San Francisco: Jossey-Bass, 2006).

In other words, who you are in the pulpit is at least as important as what you say. Is it the seminary's proper role to be involved in personhood development? How must seminaries and ecclesial bodies work together in spiritual and character formation of ministerial candidates? What approaches to personhood development might be helpful? These are questions that remain to be answered through further research.

At the core of *Poet-Gardener* lies the conviction that preaching is a relational enterprise. Certainly, preparing and delivering sermons involves competency in key tasks of preaching. And yet, all of the techniques and methods of preaching work in service of relationships. One might say that the preacher's "relational intelligence" is a key factor in his or her preaching effectiveness. What implications does this notion hold for theological education?

Ironically, *Poet-Gardener* commends the importance of relational competence to an educational sub-culture that views relationships as something other than the core process of learning. Henri Nouwen's critique of modern educational environments characterizes them as "reactive and violent" systems that major in competition and fear-based didactics. He suggests that theological education needs a paradigm shift to a "redemptive" model of learning in which relationships, not graded performance, are at the center.[328] I couldn't agree more.

From the perspective of research, paradigm shifts are easier to commend than implement. Many systemic influences conspire to maintain a secular higher education approach to theological education. The Association for Theological Schools acknowledges that ministers need attention to relational skills as part of their training.

---

[328] Henri Nouwen, *Creative Ministry*, 22-29.

Even so, relational skills are subsumed in accreditation standards under field education and pastoral theology as part of a larger curriculum.

Over the past several years, seminaries have shown growing interest in developing a more relational approach to education. In *Faithful to the Call,* Melissa Wiginton summarizes a consultation with churches and seminaries across North America conducted by the Fund for Theological Education. Through the course of this consultation, certain attributes of effective ministers repeatedly surfaced. In citing a list of ten key attributes of effective ministers, Wiginton underlines the importance of relational competence. Four out of ten of the listed attributes relate directly to relational skills.[329] Clearly, church and seminary recognize that ministry is fundamentally relational enterprise. Nowhere is this truer than in the pulpit.

Even so, relational emphases in theological education are at the "dawning awareness" stage. There seems to be little agreement about best practices for pastoral training that might enhance students' relational intelligence. Theological field education is a venue in which more intentional research ought be done to identify best practices and learning environments that promote relational theology. Especially where preaching is concerned, the minister's early experiences deeply influence anxiety levels and expectations for future congregational ministry. Partnerships with local congregations that provide students with regular opportunities to preach in a loving, encouraging environment would go a long way toward fostering more relational preaching.

Full Circle

---

[329] Melissa Wiginton, *Faithful to the Call: A Report on Consultations by the Fund for Theological Education* (Atlanta: The Fund for Theological Education, 2006), 22-23.

And so, *Poet-Gardener* has come full circle. I began this work with reflections on my own life changing experience through a sermon. *Poet-Gardener* has turned over many stones looking for ways to preach that might offer others the same kind of transformative experience. The human temptation is to look for a "silver bullet," a preaching strategy that will win souls and change hearts. In the end, we are left with the voice of God. As the following poem suggests, listening for the voice of God turns out to be the most joyful and satisfying experience of all.

The Voice
(Psalm 29)
The Voice speaks in every tongue and none
The Voice in thunder,
Windstorms, lightning, and one
Ruby-throat hummingbird's tiny, hovering hum
The Voice all around and deep within
Inviting, entreating beyond the din
Of whirring thoughts and pressing deadlines
The Voice speaking now and for all time:
    "You are My beloved, My personal delight
You are My child, a joy in My sight
You are My hope that this world still might hear
My Voice of unending love, ever speaking
Distant echo, very near.[330]

---

[330] Guy R. Brewer, *Poems, Prayers, and Promises* (Sweet Briar, VA: Sweet Briar Publications, 2006).

BIBLIOGRAPHY

Achebe, Chinua. *Things Fall Apart.* New York: Anchor Books, 1994.

Adams, Jay E. *Competent to Counsel.* Nashville: P and R Publishing, 1970.

Aden, LeRoy H. and Robert G. *Preaching God's Compassion: Comforting Those Who Suffer.* Minneapolis: Fortress Press, 2002.

Ailes, Roger. *You Are The Message.* New York: Doubleday, 1995.

Allen, Ronald. J. *Patterns of Preaching: A Sermon Sampler.* St. Louis, Missouri: Chalice Press, 1998.

Allen, Ronald J. and John C. Holbert. *Holy Root, Holy Branches: Christian Preaching from the Old Testament.* Nashville: Abingdon Press, 1995.

Alling, Roger. and David J. Schlafer, (eds.). *Preaching as the Art of Sacred Conversations: Sermons That Work.* Harrisburg, PA: Morehouse Publishing, 1997.

Aristotle. *Rhetoric.* Translated by Rhys W. Roberts, London: Kessinger Publishing, 2004.

Aristotle. "De Interpretatione", 16a, in *The Basic Works of Aristotle,* edited by R. McKeon. New York: Random House, 1941.

Attfield, D.G. "I in You and You in Me: Perichoresis and Salvation." *Theology,* 109, no. 852 (November/December, 2006): 421-429.

Auden, W. H. and Edward Mendelson. *Collected Poems (Modern Library)* New York: Random House, 2007.

Augsburger, David. *Dissident Discipleship: A Spirituality of Self-Surrender, Love of God, and Love of Neighbor.* Grand Rapids, MI: Brazos Press, 2006.

Augsburger, Myron S. "Preaching Evangelistically." http://www.christianitytoday.com, 2009 (accessed July 1, 2009).

Augustine, Aurelius. *The Confessions of St. Augustine.* Modern English Version. Grand Rapids: Revell, 2008.

Bacon, Francis and Michael Kiernan. *The Advancement of Learning: Modern Library Science).* New York: Random House, 2001.

Barclay, William. *The Letters to the Galatians and Ephesians.* Louisville: Westminster John Knox, 2002.

_____ *The Gospel of Luke.* Louisville: Westminster John Knox Press, 2001.

Barrett, C.K. *The First Epistle to Corinthians.* Peabody, MA: Hendrickson Publishers, 1993.

_____ *A Commentary on the Second Epistle to the Corinthians.* Peabody, MA: Hendrickson, 1987.

Benner, David G. *Care of Souls: Revisioning Christian Nurture and Counsel.* Grand Rapids, MI: Baker Books, 1998.

_____ "The Incarnation as a Metaphor for Psychotherapy," *Journal of Psychology and Theology,* 1983, 11, no. 4, (1983): 287-294.

Benner, David G. and Lawrence J. Crabb. *Sacred Companions: The Gift of Spiritual Direction and Friendship.* Downers Grove, IL: InterVarsity Press, 2002.

Bonhoeffer, Dietrich. *Letters and Papers from Prison.* New York: Touchstone, 1997.

_____ *Life Together.* New York: HarperOne, 1978.

Bonsignor, John J. "In Parables: Teaching Through Parables." *Legal Studies Forum,* 12, no. 1, (1988): 1-15.

Boyd, Jeffrey H. *Reclaiming the Soul: The Search for Meaning in a Self-Centered Society.* Cleveland, Ohio: Pilgrim Press, 1996.

Bozarth-Campbell, Ella. *The Word's Body: An Incarnational Aesthetic of Interpretation.* Tuscaloosa, Alabama: University of Alabama Press, 1979.

Brand, Paul and Philip Yancey. *Fearfully and Wonderfully Made.* Grand Rapids, MI: Zondervan, 1997.

Brewer, Guy R. "METAMORPH Integrative Christian Counseling Grid." Class Lecture, Anderson School of Theology, Anderson, IN, September, 2005.

_____ *Poems, Prayers, and Promises.* Sweet Briar, VA: Sweet Briar Publications, 2006.

_____ "Murph the Surf Comes to Preach." Interview of attendees of United Methodist Men's Retreat, Leesburg, FL, October, 1991.

Brewer, Jed D. "The I Don't Get It Minute." Sermon, The Bridge Ministry, Chicago, IL, July, 2009.

_____ "Welcome Home. *"Mission USA Productions Newsletter*. June, 2009, http://www.missionusa.org (accessed June 21, 2009).

Brooks, Phillips. *The Joy of Preaching*, Grand Rapids, Michigan: Kregel Publications, 1989.

Brother Lawrence, *The Practice of the Presence of God and the Spiritual Maxims*. New York: Cosimo Books, 2006.

Brown, Michael L. "In the End." Sermon, Brownsville Assembly of God Church, Pensacola, Florida, October, 1999.

Brown, Raymond E. *The Gospel According to John, I-XII*. Anchor Bible Series Volume 29. New York: Bantam Doubleday, 1966.

_____ *The Gospel According to John, XIII-XXI*. Anchor Bible Series Volume 30. New Haven: Yale University Press, 1970.

Browing, Don S. *The Moral Context of Pastoral Care*. Philadelphia: Westminster Press, 1976.

Brueggemann, Walter. *The Prophetic Imagination*. Philadelphia: Fortress Press, 2001.

_____. *Texts Under Negotiation*. Augsburg Fortress, Minneapolis, MN., 1993.

_____ *Finally Comes the Poet*. Augsburg Fortress, Minneapolis, MN.,1989.

Brueggemann, Walter, William Placher, and Brian Blount. *Struggling with Scripture*. London: Westminster John Knox Press, 2002.

Bryant, David J. *Faith and the Play of Imagination: On the Role of Imagination in Religion*. Macon, Georgia: Mercer University Press, 1989.

Buber, Martin. *Werke: Zweiter Band Schriften zur Bible. Band 2,* vol. 3. In *Care of Souls: Revisioning Christian Nurture and Counsel*. Grand Rapids, MI: Baker Books, 1998.

Bullock, Jeffrey F. "Preaching in a Postmodern World: Gadamer's Philosophical Hermeneutics as a Homiletical Conversation." Christian Theological Research Group, http://www.apu.edu/-CTRF/papers/1997 (accessed date April 6, 2004).

Buttrick, David. *Homiletic Moves and Structures*. Fortress Press, Philadelphia, 1987.

Buxton, Graham. *The Trinity, Creation, and Pastoral Ministry.* Carlisle: Paternoster, 2005.

Calvin, John. *Institutes of the Christian Religion,* Book 1, Chaps 11-12. Library of Christian Classics 22, edited by John T. McNeill. Translated by Ford Lewis Battles. Philadelphia: Westminster Press, 1960.

Campbell, Alastair V. "Wise Folly," in *Rediscovering Pastoral Care,* 55-71. Philadelphia:Westminster, 1981.

Capps, Donald. "The Wise Fool Reframes," in *Reframing: A New Method in Pastoral Care,* 1-8 and169-182. Minneapolis: Fortress Press, 1990.

Carrell, Lori. *The Great American Sermon Survey.* Wheaton, Illinois: Mainstay Church Resources, 2000.

Challies, Tim. *The Discipline of Spiritual Discernment.* Wheaton, Illinois: Crosssway Books, 2007.

Chandler, Steven. "Incarnational Ministry," *Encounter, Journal for Pentecostal Ministry,* 3, no. 1, (Summer 2006).

Chappel, Bryan. *Christ-Centered Preaching: Redeeming the Expository Sermon.* Grand Rapids, MI: Baker Academic, 2004.

Cho, David Yonggi. *The Fourth Dimension, Volume II.* Gainesville, Florida: Bridge-Logos Publishers, 2002.

Churchill, Winston. "The Actions of Russia," BBC Radio broadcast, October, 1939. http://www.phrases.org.uk/meanings/31000.html (accessed January 11, 2009).

Clark, William R. and Michael Grunstein. *Are We Hardwired? The Role of Genes in Human Behavior.* New York: Oxford Press, 2004.

Clebsch, William A. and Charles R. Jaekle. *Pastoral Care in Historical Perspective.* Englewood Cliffs, New Jersey: Prentice-Hall, 1964.

Cobb, Jon B., Jr. *Grace and Responsibility: A Wesleyan Theology for Today.* Nashville: Abingdon Press, 1995.

Cole, Graham. "Preaching Christ in a Postmodern World." *Perspective,* 8, no. 1 (2000). http://www.perspective.org.au (accessed date August 6, 2008).

Coleridge, Samuel Taylor. *Critical Theory Since Plato.* Edited by Hazard Adams.New York: Harcourt Brace Janovich, 1971.

Collins, Kenneth J. *Exploring Christian Spirituality: An Ecumenical Reader*. Grand Rapids, MI: Baker Academic, 2000.

_____ *Soul Care: Deliverance and Renewal Through the Christian Life*. Grand Rapids, MI: Victor Books, 1995.

Cooper, Burton Z. and McClure, John S. *Claiming Theology in the Pulpit*. Louisville: Westminster John Knox Press, 2003.

Cosgrove, Charles H., Dow W. Edgerton, and Don M. Wardlaw. *In Other Words: Incarnational Translation for Preaching*. Grand Rapids, MI: William B. Eerdmans Publishing, 2007.

Cox, Harvey G. *The Secular City: Secularization and Urbanization in Theological Perspective*. New York: Collier, 1990.

Crabb, Lawrence J. *Inside Out*. Colorado Springs, Colorado: NavPress Publications, 2007.

Craddock, Fred B. *As One Without Authority*. New York: Christian Board of Publication, 2001.

_____ *Luke*. Interpretation, A Bible Commentary for Teaching and Preaching. Louisville: Westminster John Knox Press, 1991.

_____ *Overhearing the Gospel*. New York: Chalice Press, 2002.

_____ *Preaching*. Nashville: Abingdon Press, 2010.

Crawford, Evans. *The Hum*. Abingdon Preachers Library. Nashville: Abingdon, 1995.

Cross, F.L. and E.A. Livingstone, E. A. eds. *The Oxford Dictionary of the Christian Church*. New York: Oxford University Press, 2005.

Dayringer, Richard. *The Heart of Pastoral Counseling: Healing Through Relationship*. Binghampton, NY: Haworth Press, Inc., 1998.

De Caussade, Jean-Pierre. *Abandonment to Divine Providence*. Translated by John Beevers. New York: Doubleday, 1975.

Derrida, Jacques and Alan Bass. *Positions*. Chicago: The University of Chicago Press, 1981.

Dervin, Brenda. "Information as a User Construct: The Relevance of Perceived Information Needs to Synthesis and Interpretation," in *Knowledge Structure and Use: Implications for Synthesis and*

Interpretation. Edited by S. A. Ward and L. J. Reed (Philadelphia, PA: Temple University Press, 1983), 160.

Dodd, C.H. *The Apostolic Preaching and Its Developments: Three Lectures with an Eschatology and History*. New York: Harper and Row, 1964.

Dostoevsky, Fyodor. *The Idiot*. Trans. David Magershack. New York: Penguin, 1955.

Dykstra, Robert C., ed. *Images of Pastoral Care: Classic Readings*. St. Louis: Chalice, 2005.

Edwards, Jonathan. *Sinners in the Hands of an Angry God*. Pensacola, FL: Christian Life Books, 2003.

Elliot, Elisabeth. *Shadow of the Almighty: The Life and Testament of Jim Elliot (Lives of Faith)*. New York: HarperOne, 1989.

Elmore, Tim. "A New Kind of Leader: Leading Effectively as Our Culture Evolves." Growing Leaders. http://www.growingleaders.com (accessed date July 2, 2008).

Elmore, Tim. *Intentional Influence*. Nashville: Lifeway Press, 2003.

Entralgo, Pedro Lain. *The Therapy of the Word in Classical Antiquity*. New Haven: Yale University Press, 1970.

Entwistle, David N. *Integrative Approaches to Psychology and Christianity: An Introduction to Worldview Issues, Philosophical Foundations, and Models of Integration*. Eugene, OR: Wipf and Stock Publishers, 2004.

Eswine, Zack. *Preaching To A Post-Everything World: Crafting Biblical Sermons That Connect with Our Culture*. Grand Rapids, MI: Baker Books, 2008.

Eslinger, Richard L. *The Web of Preaching*. Abingdon Press, Nashville, TN, 2002.

Estes, Clarisa Pinkola. *Women Who Run with the Wolves*. New York: Ballantine Books, 1996.

Gillian R. Evans, "On the Steps of Humility and Pride," *Bernard of Clairvaux: Selected Works,* The Classics of Western Spirituality (Mahwah, N.J.: Paulist Press, 1987.

Faber, Heije. "The Minister in the Hospital," in *Pastoral Care in the Modern Hospital,* , 81-92.Translated by Hugo DeWaal. Philadelphia: Westminster, 1971.

Festinger, L., S. Schachter, S., and K. Back. *Social Pressure in Informal Groups*. Palo Alto, CA: Stanford University Press, 1950.

Fiddes, Paul S. *Participating in the Life of God: A Pastoral Doctrine of the Trinity.* London: Darton, Longman, and Todd, 2000.

Fitzmeyer, Joseph A. *The Gospel According to Luke I-IX.* Anchor Bible Series, vol. 28. New York: Doubleday, 1981.

Foster, Charles R., Lisa E. Dahill, Lawrence A. Golemon, and Barbara Wang Tolentino. *Educating Clergy: Teaching Practices and Pastoral Imagination.* San Francisco: Jossey-Bass, 2006.

Foster, Richard J. *Prayer: Finding the Heart's True Home.* San Francisco: Harper-Collins, 2007.

Fowler, James A. *Evangelical Humanism.* Dallas: Lighthouse Library International, 1999.

Frei, Hans W. *The Eclipse of Biblical Narrative,* New Haven: Yale Univ. Press, 1974.

Frymer-Kinsey, Tikya. *Christianity in Jewish Terms.* New York: Basic Books, 2002.

Gadamer, Hans-Georg, Joel Weinsheimer, and Donald G. Marshall. *Truth and Method.* London: Continuum Publishers, 2004.

Gardner, Howard. *Changing Minds.* Boston: Harvard Business School Press, 2004.

Geisler, Norman F. and William E. Nix. *A General Introduction to the Bible.* "Definitions of Revelation and Inspiration." Chicago: Moody Press, 1986.

Gibbs, Eddie. *ChurchNext: Quantum Changes in How We Do Ministry.* Downers Grove, IL: InterVarsity Press, 2000.

Gibbs, Eddie, and Ryan K. Bolger. *Emerging Churches: Creating Christian Community in Postmodern Cultures.* Grand Rapids, MI: Baker Academic, 2005.

Gilbert, Daniel. *Stumbling on Happiness.* New York: Vintage Press, 2007.

Graham, Billy. "You Have a Hole in Your Heart." Sermon, Jacksonville, Florida, February, 1999.

Green, Garrett. *Imagining God: Theology and the Religious Imagination.* San Francisco: Harper and Row, 1989.

Gregory the Great. *Pastoral Care.* Ancient Christian Writers Series, vol. 11. Translated by Henry D. Davis. Mahwah, NJ: Paulist Press, 1978.

Gunton, Colin E. "Relation and Relativity: The Trinity and the Created World" in

Trinitarian Theology Today: Essays on Divine Being and Act, 91-112. Edited by Christoph Schwobel. Edinburgh: T. and T. Clark, 1995.

_____ *The One, The Three, and The Many.* Cambridge: Cambridge University Press, 1993.

Hadaway, C. Kirk and Roozen, David A. *Rerouting the Protestant Mainstream: Sources of Growth and Opportunities for Change.* Nashville: Abingdon, 1994.

Hall, Douglas John. *Lighten Our Darkness.* Philadelphia: Westminster, 1976.

Hamilton, Barry W. "A Model for Teaching Research Methods in Theological Education." Northeastern Seminary, Rochester, New York. http://www.*acc.roberts.edu*/Hamilton_Barry/A%20MODEL%20FOR%20TEACHING%20RESEARCH%. (accessed July 30, 2009).

Harding, Joe. *Have I Told You Lately? Preaching to Help People and Churches Grow.* Nashville: Church Growth Press, 1986.

Hartshorne, Charles. *The Divine Relativity: A Social Conception of God (The Terry Lecture Series).* New Haven: Yale University Press, 1982.

Heath, Dan and Heath, Chip. *Made To Stick: Why Some Ideas Survive and Others Die.* New York: Random House, 2007.

Hebblethwaite, Brian. *The Incarnation: Collected Essays in Christology.* Cambridge: Cambridge University Press, 1987.

Heisler, Greg. *Spirit-led Preaching: The Holy Spirit's Role in Sermon Preparation and Delivery.* Nashville: B and H Publishing Company, 2007.

Hernandez, Wil. *Henri Nouwen and Soul Care: A Ministry of Integration.* Mahwah, NJ: Paulist Press, 2008.

Hilkert, Mary Catherine. *Naming Grace: Preaching and the Sacramental Imagination.* New York: Continuum, 1997.

Hillman, George M., Jr. *Ministry Greenhouse: Cultivating Environments for Practical Learning.* Herndon, VA: The Alban Institute, 2008.

Hiltner, Seward, "The Solicitous Shepherd," in *Images of Pastoral Care: Classic Readings,* 47-53. Edited by Robert Dykstra. St. Louis: Chalice Press, 2005.

Holmes, Urban T. *A History of Christian Spirituality.* New York: Seabury, 1980.

Hugo Victor, *Les Miserables.* Modern Library Edition, New York: Random House, 1992.

Hunt, Earl G. "Selfish Ambition." Lecture, Lakeland First United Methodist Church, Lakeland, FL, May, 1987.

Hunter, George G. III. *Church for the Unchurched.* Nashville: Abingdon, 1996.

Jeremias, Joachim. *The Parables of Jesus.* New York: Charles Scribner's Sons, 1963.

John Chrysostom. *St. Chrysostom's Homilies on the Gospel of John and Hebrews: Nicene and Post-Nicene Fathers of the Christian Church, Part 14,* Whitefish, MT: Kessinger Publishing, 2004.

John of Damascus. *On the Divine Images: Three Apologies Against Those Who Attack the Divine Images.* Translated by David Anderson. Crestwood, NY: St. Vladimir's Seminary Press, 1980.

Jones, Kirk Byron. *The Jazz of Preaching: How to Preach with Great Freedom and Joy.* Nashville: Abingdon Press, 2004.

Kafka, Franz. "Selections from Letters to Friends," in *The Basic Kafka.* New York: Pocket Books, 1984.

Kalas, J. Ellsworth. *Preaching from the Soul.* Abingdon Press: Nashville, TN, 2003.

Kearney, Richard. *Poetics of Imagining: From Husserl to Lyotard.* New York: Harper Collins Academic, 1991.

Kegan, Robert. *The Evolving Self: Problem and Process in Human Development.* Cambridge, Massachusetts: Harvard University Press, 1982.

Kenneson, Philip D. *Life on the Vine: Cultivating the Fruit of the Spirit in Christian Community.* Downers Grove: InterVarsity Press, 1999.

Kierkegaard, Soren. *Concluding Unscientific Postscript.* Princeton, NJ: Princeton University Press, 1968.

_____ *Point of View of My Work as an Author.* Translated by Walter Lowrie. New York: Harper Torchbooks, 1962.

Kierkegaard, Soren and Thomas C. Oden. *Parables of Kierkegaard (Kierkegaard's Writings).* Princeton, New Jersey: Princeton University Press, 1978.

Kimball, Dan. *The Emerging Church: Vintage Christianity for New Generations.* Grand Rapids, MI: Zondervan, 2003.

_____. *Emerging Worship: Creating New Worship Gatherings for Emerging Generations*. Grand Rapids, MI: Zondervan, 2004.

King, Martin Luther, Jr. "A Knock at Midnight," in *King Came Preaching* by Mervyn A. Warren. Downers Grove, IL: InterVarsity Press, 2001.

_____ "A Tough Mind and a Tender Heart." in *King Came Preaching* by Mervyn A. Warren, Downers Grove, IL: InterVarsity Press, 2001.

_____ "The I have a dream speech," http://www.usconstitution.net/dream, 2006, (accessed July 20, 2009).

Kinlaw, Dennis F. *Let's Start with Jesus: A New Way of Doing Theology*. Grand Rapids: Zondervan, 2005.

_____ *Preaching in the Spirit: A Preacher Looks for Something That Human Energy Cannot Provide*. Wilmore, KY: Francis Asbury Society, 1985.

Knowles, Michael P. *The Folly of Preaching: Models and Methods*. Grand Rapids, MI: William B. Eerdmans, 2007.

Kohut, Heinz.. *The Analysis of the Self*. New York: International Universities Press, 1971.

Kornfeld, Margaret. *Cultivating Wholeness: A Guide to Care and Counseling in Faith Communities*. New York: Continuum, 2006.

Korzenny, Felipe. "A Theory of Electronic Propinquity: Mediated Communication in Organizations." *Communication Research,* 5, No.1, (January 1978): 3-24.

Kysar, Robert and Joseph M. Webb. *Preaching to Postmoderns: New Perspectives for Proclaiming the Message*. Peabody, Massachusetts: Hendrickson Publishers, 2006.

LaCugna, Catherine Mowry. *God For Us: The Trinity and Christian Life*. San Francisco: HarperCollins, 1991.

Lamott, Anne. *Bird by Bird: Some Instructions on Writing and Life*. New York: Anchor, 1995.

Larkin, Earnest E. "The Three Spiritual Ways." International Order of Carmelites. http: www.carmelnet.org, 2008 (accessed March 16, 2009).

Leech, Kenneth. *Soul Friend*. San Francisco: Harper and Row, 1977.

Lewis, C.S. *The Four Loves*. New York: Harcourt Brace, 1960.

_____ *The Weight of Glory.* New York: HarperOne, 2001.

Lischer, Richard. *The End of Words: The Language of Reconciliation in a Culture of Violence (Lyman Beecher Lectures in Preaching).* Grand Rapids, MI: William B. Eerdmans, 2005.

Long, Jimmy. *Emerging Hope: A Strategy for Reaching the Postmodern Generations.* Downers Grove, IL: Intervarsity Press, 2004.

Long, Thomas G. *The Witness of Preaching.* Louisville: Westminster John Knox Press, 1990.

Lorenz, Konrad. *On Aggression.* New York: Bantam Books, 1971.

Lowe, Robert. *Improvisation, Inc.: Harnessing Spontaneity to Engage People and Groups.* San Francisco: Jossey-Bass/Pfeiffer, 2000.

Lowry, Eugene L. *The Homiletical Plot: The Sermon as Narrative Art Form.* Louisville: Westminster John Knox Press, 2001.

Lyotard, Jean-Francois. *The Postmodern Condition: A Report on Knowledge (Theory and History of Literature, vol. X).* Minneapolis: University of Minnesota Press, 1984.

Marcel, Gabriel. *The Mystery of Being: Faith and Reality, Volume 2.* New York: Lanham, 1951.

Marty, Martin. "The Long Road to Reconciliation," *Newsweek,* 27 (March 2000): 61.

May, Gerald G. *Addiction and Grace: Love and Spirituality in the Healing of Addictions.* New York: HarperOne, 2007.

_____ *Will and Spirit: A Contemplative Psychology.* San Francisco: Harper and Row, 1982.

McClure, John S. *Other-wise Preaching: A Postmodern Ethics for Homiletics.* St. Louis: Chalice Press, 2001.

McDowell, Josh. *Evidence for Christianity.* Nashville: Thomas Nelson Publishers, 2006.

McMinn, Mark. *Psychology, Theology, and Spirituality in Christian Counseling.* Philadelphia: Tyndale House, 1996.

McNeill, John. *A History of the Cure of Souls.* New York: Harper Collins, 1977.

Melancthon, Philip. *Melancthon and Bucer.* Library of Christian

Classics. Edited by Wilhelm Pauck. Philadelphia: Westminster Press, 1969.

Menninger, Karl. *Whatever Became of Sin?* New York: Bantam Books, 1978,

Mitchell, J.T.W., ed. *The Language of Images.* Chicago: University of Chicago Press, 1980.

Mitchell, Jolyon P. *Visually Speaking: Radio and The Renaissance of Preaching.* Louisville: Wesminster John Knox Press, 1999.

Moltmann, Jürgen. *Experiences in Theology: Ways and Forms of Christian Theology.* Minneapolis: Fortress Press, 2000.

Moon, Gary W. and David G. Benner. *Spiritual Direction and the Care of Souls: A Guide to Christian Approaches and Practices.* Downers Grove, IL: InterVarsity Press, 2004.

Moore, Sonia. *The Stanislavski System: The Professional Training of an Actor.* New York: Penguin Books, Inc., 1984.

Moore, Thomas. *Care of the Soul: A Guide for Cultivating Depth and Sacredness in Everyday Life.* New York: Harper Collins Publishers, 1992.

Murray, Andrew. *The Fruit of the Vine.* New York: T.Y. Crowell and Co., 1898.

Murray, Edward L. *Phenomenological Psychology.* Pittsburgh: Duquesne University Press, 1987.

Murphy, Jack Roland. *Jewels for the Journey.* New York: International Prison Ministry, 1990.

Muto, Susan. *Pathways of Spiritual Living.* Pittsburgh: Epiphany Books, 2006.

Narramore, S. Bruce. *No Condemnation: Rethinking Guilt Motivation in Counseling, Preaching, and Parenting.* Eugene, OR: Resource Publications, 2002.

Nichols, J. Randall. *The Restoring Word: Preaching as Pastoral Communication.* New York: Harper and Row, 1987.

Niebuhr, Richard H. *Christ and Culture.* New York: Harper and Brothers Publishers, 1951.

_____ *The Meaning of Revelation,* New York: Macmillan, 1941.

Nouwen, Henri, *Creative Ministry.* New York: Image Books, 1991.

_____ *In the Name of Jesus: Reflections on Christian Leadership.* New York: Crossroad Publishing Company, 1993.

_____ *Life of the Beloved: Spiritual Living in a Secular World.* New York: Crossroad Publishing Company, 2002.

_____ *Lifesigns: Intimacy, Fecundity, and Ecstasy in Christian Perspective.* New York: Doubleday, 1991.

_____ *Reaching Out: The Three Movements of the Spiritual Life.* New York: Doubleday, 1975.

_____ *Return of the Prodigal Son.* New York: Crossroads, 1996.

_____ *Spiritual Direction: Wisdom for the Long Walk of Faith.* New York: Harper One, 2006.

_____ *The Wounded Healer.* New York: Doubleday, 1979.

Oden, Thomas C. *Care of Souls in the Classic Tradition.* Philadelphia: Fortress Press, 1984.

Ong, Walter. *The Presence of the word: Some Prolegomena for cultural and religious History.* New Haven: Yale University Press, 1967.

Ortberg, John. *The Life You've Always Wanted.* Grand Rapids, MI: Zondervan, 2002.

Otto, Randall E. "The Use and Abuse of Perichoresis in Recent Theology." *Scottish Journal of Theology,"* 54, no 1,(2001): 366-384.

Pargament, Kenneth. *The Psychology of Religion and Coping: Theory, Research, and Practice.* New York: The Guilford Press, 2001.

Parks, Sharon Daloz. *The Critical Years.: Young Adults and the Search for Meaning, Faith, and Commitment.* San Francisco: Harper Collins, 1991.

Pasquarello, Michael III. *Sacred Rhetoric: Classic Images for Preaching.* Grand Rapids: Zondervan, 2005.

Paulsell, Stephanie. "Praying on Paper." *Christian Century* 118, no.32, (November 21-28 (2001): 9-10.

_____ "Spiritual Formation and Intellectual Work in Theological Education," *Theology Today* 55, no. 2 (July 1998): 229-234.

Patterson, Kerry, Joseph Grenny, David Maxfield, Ron McMillan, and Al Switzler. *Influencer: The Power to Change Anything*. New York: McGraw-Hill, 2008.

Perry, William G., Jr. *Forms of Intellectual and Ethical Development in the College Years*. New York: Holt, Rinehart, and Winston, Inc., 1970.

Peterson, Eugene H. *A Long Obedience in the Same Direction: Discipleship in an Instant Society*. Downers Grove, IL: InterVarsity Press, 2000.

_____ *Christ Plays in Ten Thousand Places: A Conversation in Spiritual Theology*. Grand Rapids, MI: William B. Eerdmans, 2005.

_____ *Five Smooth Stones for Pastoral Work*. Grand Rapids, MI: William B. Eerdmans, 1992.

Peterson, Eugene H. and Dawn, Marva. *The Unnecessary Pastor: Rediscovering the Call*. Grand Rapids, MI: William B. Eerdmans, 2000.

Phillips, Rachael. *It Is Well With My Soul: Four Dramatic Stories of Great Hymn Writers*. Uhrichsville, OH: Barbour, 2004.

Plato, "Apology," in *Great Books of the Western World*. Edited by Robert Maynard Hutchings. Chicago: Encyclopedia Britannica, 1952, 7.

Post Modern Preaching. "Incarnational Preaching." http://www.postmodernpreaching,net/incarnationalpreaching (accessed date August 14, 2008.)

Principe, Walter. "Toward Defining Spirituality." in *Exploring Christian Spirituality: An Ecumenical Reader* edited by Kenneth J. Collins, 43-60. Grand Rapids, MI: Baker Academic, 2000.

Pruyser, Paul W. *The Play of the Imagination: Toward a Psychoanalysis of Culture*. New York: International Universities Press, 1983.

Rattenbury, J. Ernest. *The Conversion of the Wesleys*. London: The Epworth Press, 1938.

Richardson, Ronald W. *Creating a Healthier Church: Family Systems Theory, Leadership, and Congregational Life*. Philadelphia: Fortress Press, 1996.

Rilke, Rainer Maria. *Letters to a Young Poet*. Novato: CA: New World Library, 2006.

Rose, Lucy Atkinson. *Sharing the Word: Preaching in the Roundtable Church*. Louisville: Westminster John Knox Press, 1997.

St. Gregory Episcopal Church. "Sarx," http://raphael.doxos.com/2008/06/28/tripudiuproces sion-to-the-table-and-transfer-of-gifts, (accessed August 20, 2009)./

Sample, Tex. *The Spectacle of Worship in a Wired World.* Nashville: Abingdon Press, 1998.

Scazzero, Peter. *The Emotionally Healthy Church: A Strategy for Discipleship that Actually Changes Lives.* Grand Rapids, MI: Zondervan, 2003.

Schwarz, Christian A. *Natural Church Development: A Guide to Eight Essential Qualities of Healthy Churches.* St. Charles, IL: ChurchSmart Resources, 1996.

Shaddix, Jim. *The Passion-Driven Sermon: Changing the Way Pastors Preach and Congregations Listen.* Nashville: Broadman and Holman, 2003.

Stanley, Scott M. and Gary Smalley. *The Power of Commitment: A Guide to Active, Lifelong Love.* San Francisco: Jossey-Bass, 2005.

Reconstructionist Synagogue, Princeton, New Jersey. http://www.Stringofpearlsweb.org. (accessed date March 4, 2009).

Strong, James. *Strong's Exhaustive Concordance of the Bible.* Nashville: Thomas Nelson, 1996.

Sweet, Leonard I., and Andy Crouch. *The Church in Emerging Culture: Five Perspectives.* El Cajon, CA: Youth Specialties, 2003.

Tannen, Deborah. *The Argument Culture: Moving from Debate to Dialogue.* New York: Random House, 1998.

Tekyl, Terry. *Making Room to Pray.* Anderson, IN: Bristol, 1999.

Tenney, Tommy. *God's Eye View: Worshipping Your Way to a Higher Perspective.* Nashville: Thomas Nelson Publishers, 2002.

Tozer, A.W. *The Knowledge of the Holy: The Attributes of God and Their Meaning in The Christian Life.* New York: HarperOne, 1992.

Troeger, Thomas G. "Imaginative Theology: The Shape of Postmodern Homiletics," *Homiletic* 13, no. 1 (1988): 21-34.

_____ "Staying Alive in the Pulpit!" Part IV of *Imagination and Metaphor In Preaching.* Nashville: Ecufilms, 2001.

Van Gelder, Craig. *The Essence of the Church: A Community Created by the Spirit*

Grand Rapids, MI: Baker Books, 2000.

Van Kaam, Adrian and Susan Muto. *Am I Living a Spiritual Life?* Pittsburgh: Sophia Institute Press, 2006.

Vine, W. E. *Vine's Expository Dictionary of Old and New Testament Words.* Nashville: Thomas Nelson, 2003.

Volf, Miroslav and Bass, Dorothy C. *Practicing Theology: Beliefs and Practices in Christian Life.* Grand Rapids, MI: William B. Eerdmans, 2002.

Ware, Corinne. *Discover Your Spiritual Type.* Herndon, Virginia: The Alban Institute, 1995.

Warren, Mervyn A. *King Came Preaching: The Pulpit Power of Dr. Martin Luther King, Jr.* Downers Grove, IL: InterVarsity Press, 2001.

Warnock, Mary. *Imagination.* Berkeley: University of California Press, 1976.

Webb, Joseph M. *Comedy and Preaching.* St. Louis, Missouri: Chalice Press, 1998.

_____ *Preaching Without Notes.* Nashville: Abingdon Press, 2001.

Webber, Robert E. *Ancient-Future Faith: Rethinking Evangelicalism for a Post-Modern World.* Grand Rapids, MI: Baker Academic, 1999.

Wesley, John and Collins, Kenneth J.. "On Working Out Our Own Salvation" (Sermon #85) in *Wesley on Salvation: A Study in the Standard Sermons.* Grand Rapids, MI: Zondervan, 1989.

Wesley, John *The Works of John Wesley, Volume 11, No. 29.* Edited by Thomas Jackson. Grand Rapids, MI: Baker Books, 1996.

Wesley, John and Albert C. Outler. *John Wesley (Library of Protestant Thought).* New York: Oxford University Press, 1980.

Westerhoff, John. *Spiritual Life: The Foundation for Preaching and Teaching.* Louisville: Westminster John Knox Press, 1994.

Wheelwright, Phillip. *The Burning Fountain: A Study in the Language of Symbolism.* Bloomington, IN: Indiana University Press, 1968.

Wiginton, Melissa. *Faithful to the Call: A Report on Consultations by the Fund for Theological Education.* Atlanta: The Fund for Theological Education, 2006.

Willard, Dallas. *Hearing God: Developing a Conversational Relationship with God.* Downers Grove, IL: InterVarsity, 1999.

Williams, Thomas. "Saint Anselm," *The Stanford Dictionary of Philosophy (Fall 2008 Edition).* Edited by Edward N. Zalta. http://plato.stanford.edu/archives/fall2008/entries/anselm/ (accessed July 3, 2008).

Willimon, William H. *Pastor: The Theology and Practice of Ordained Ministry.* Nashville: Abingdon Press, 2002.

Wills, Dick. *Waking to God's Dream: Spiritual Leadership and Church Renewal.* Nashville: Abingdon, 1999.

Wilson, Paul Scott. *The Four Pages of the Sermon: A Guide to Biblical Preaching.* Nashville: Abingdon Press, 1999.

Witherington, Ben III. *The Gospel of Mark: A Socio-Rhetorical Commentary.* Grand Rapids, Michigan: William B. Eerdmans Publishing Company, 2001.

Worthington, Everett L. *Forgiving and Reconciling: Bridges to Wholeness and Hope.* Downers Grove: IL: InterVarsity, 2003.

Wrede, William. *The Messianic Secret.* Translated by J.C. Grieg. Cambridge: James Clarke and Company, Ltd., 1971.

Wright, John W. *Telling God's Story: Narrative Preaching for Christian Formation.* Downers Grove, IL: InterVarsity Press, 2007.

Wright, Wendy M. *Seasons of a Family's Life: Cultivating the Contemplative Spirit at Home.* San Francisco: Jossey-Bass, 2003.

Yancey, Philip. *What's So Amazing About Grace?* Grand Rapids, MI: Zondervan, 1997.

Yerkes, Robert M. and Dodson, J.D. "The relation of strength of stimulus to rapidity of habit-formation." *Journal of Comparative Neurology and Psychology*, 18. (1908): 459-482.

Zodhiates, Spiro. *The Complete Word Study Dictionary of the New Testament.* Chattanooga, TN: AMG Publishers, 1992.

Made in the USA
Lexington, KY
29 May 2014